Understan
Industry

Alasdair Hogarth

Edward Arnold

© Alasdair Hogarth 1983
First published 1983
by Edward Arnold (Publishers) Ltd
41 Bedford Square London WC1B 3DQ

British Library Cataloguing in Publication Data

Hogarth, Alasdair
  Understanding Industry.
  1. Industry
  I. Title
  338   HD2328

ISBN 0-7131-0813-4

Text set in 12/13 pt English Times Compugraphic
by Colset Private Limited, Singapore
Printed and bound in Great Britain by Spottiswoode Ballantyne Limited,
Colchester and London

Contents

Teachers' notes

Understanding Industry is designed to be used in a variety of different ways.

It provides a self-contained course to introduce students to our industrial society in a progressive way from an introduction to a consideration of some more complex concepts and issues. Each chapter contains a number of varied questions and suggestions for follow-up work both within and outside class, to aid and increase understanding of the text.

Alternatively, each chapter can be used as a starting point with the particular topic covered, expanded by resources provided by the teacher, perhaps including films, speakers or visits.

In addition, each chapter is itself self-contained, allowing particular topics to be covered, perhaps as a part of some other course.

'We have no more right to consume
happiness without producing it
than to consume wealth without
producing it.'
    George Bernard Shaw *Candida*

Acknowledgements

The publishers would like to thank the following for their permission to reproduce copyright illustrations:-
The Science Museum, Crown Copyright Reserve pp 15, 18, 21b, 231, 25. British Leyland Limited, pp 3 & 70b. Science Museum pp 12, 21t & 23rt. Amey Roadstone Corp. Ltd. p 37. Ferranti Archives p 66t. Mullard Ltd. p 66b. Ferranti Ltd. (John Fowler Ltd.), p 67. Computer Games Ltd. p 68. Hewlett Packard Ltd. p 70t. IBM (UK) Ltd., p 71. Seiko Time (UK) Ltd., p 72. Texas Instruments, pp 73 & 74. United Nations, p 89. Marks and Spencer Plc., p 29.

1

An industrial way of life

It is easy to think of a major disaster which would completely destroy the world as we know it. A nuclear war, perhaps, or the coming of another ice age; a plague killing millions of people, or a large asteroid from space crashing into our planet. Think what it would be like if you were one of the very few people left alive after such a catastrophe. There would be no towns or cities, no electricity or water supply. There would be no doctors, hospitals or schools; no factories, cars or television. You would have to grow or catch your own food, make your own clothes, collect your own water, and find ways of keeping yourself warm and sheltered. You would have to become *self-sufficient*.

This means you make everything you need on your own, or together with your family and a few friends, instead of being able to buy things from shops. But we do not need a disaster to find people living like this. In many parts of the world it is the normal way of life. Indeed, if we could go back in time we would not need to go very far to find the people in Britain living in a self-sufficient society.

It might sound rather attractive . . .

Perhaps I'll go and hunt some deer today. Then again, I might just lie here in the sun!

Get out of bed and get to work. There's the electricity bill to pay, clothes to buy . . . . . .

2000 BC   Today

In fact, that's not a fair comparison at all. Far from being a life of idleness, life in a primitive society is a life of back-breaking toil to get enough food to eat to fend off starvation. It is a never-ending battle against the weather, the winter, natural disasters, and sometimes wild animals. There is the constant fear of illness leading usually to death or disability. You would spend most of your time being hungry, cold and worried about the future.

By comparison, in Britain today we are surrounded by untold wealth. We may work for only eight hours a day, five days a week to provide ourselves not only with food, housing and clothes, but also holidays, cars, entertainments, luxuries and a vast number of devices to make life easier and more pleasant – like washing machines, showers, books and magazines, light, central heating, films and so forth.

What is wealth?

Our way of life is the benefit we get from living in an industrial society, where we have factories and machines producing enormous numbers of articles we would have no chance of making on our own: where large numbers of people can be completely freed from making things to provide services for everyone else – services like *health, education, the post office, hairdressing and public transport.*

The amount of goods and services a society produces is called the *wealth* of that society. A few other countries, like the United States, are wealthier than Britain, because they produce more goods and services, and therefore have more to share among their population. But most countries are a great deal less wealthy than we are. So much so, that many people in the world do not even have enough to eat, far less enjoy the wide range of goods and services we take for granted. Many people think it is unfair that a few countries have so much while the rest have so little, which is why some people in Britain give money to organizations like Oxfam, the Save the Children Fund, and UNICEF, to try and help those people in poorer countries. The government too, provides money and help to assist progress in the so-called 'under-developed' or developing nations.

How do we do it?

In this book we will be looking at how it happened that Britain became a wealthy, industrial society. We will be seeing how our industrial society works, and the part each of us plays in preserving and increasing our wealth. By the end of the book you should have a much better *understanding of industry*.

British Leyland (Austin-Morris) factory, Cowley Division, Oxford

We can start by getting one thing clear about manufacturing industry. (*Manufacturing* means making things in a factory with machines.) Some industry is dirty, smelly and noisy. Some industry pollutes our air, our sea, and our land and rivers. Working in some industries can be boring, hard and unpleasant. But above everything else, our industry is the foundation of our wealth: it supports our entire way of life, with all our goods and services. Without our industry to make the goods, and therefore provide the money for the services we depend on, we would find ourselves in a very different, and a much less pleasant, society.

Now for your work

Take your workbook or folder, and write as your first title:
'Living in an industrial society'.
Try to write neatly, and in complete sentences, so that someone who does not have this book can understand what you have written and learned.

Questions

1 What is meant by the *wealth* of a society?
2 What does *manufactured* mean?
3 Make a list of all the manufactured articles which you have used today since you got up. (You might start with the alarm clock!)
4 Now go through your list and *underline* those articles which you could have made yourself. (There will be very few.) Why couldn't you have made the others? Is it that you don't know how to, that you don't have the machinery necessary, that you don't know even what they are made out of, or a combination of these?
5 Divide half of one of your pages into three columns, headed like this:

Basic needs	Self-sufficient society	Industrial society
1 Food 2 Clothes 3 Heat 4 Light 5 Shelter	Say here how each need would have been satisfied in a primitive or self-sufficient society	Say here how each need would be satisfied in an industrial society

Need we ask which way is better, more efficient, or convenient?

6 Electricity has only been in use during the last century. In this time we have come to depend on it enormously. List six essential things in the home which require electricity, and another six which require electricity but which you could happily do without. Can you remember how you were affected by a recent power cut?
7 You have been trapped by a time warp, and find yourself in the Britain of 2000 BC. How would you set about preparing yourself for the times which lie ahead?

2

The growth of money

In a *self-sufficient* society, we have seen that each family produces everything it needs itself. Each family grows its own food, makes its own clothes, collects its own water, and so on. The people produce only just enough to keep themselves alive, and sometimes not even that. They have neither the time nor the energy left over to think about doing things we would consider quite sensible, like building a stockade to protect their animals, or a barn to store food in for the winter (supposing they had some left over to store). However it would soon become obvious that some people in their small community were better at doing some things than others.

In a self-sufficient society . . .

The carpenter can't look after cattle or make clothes

The cowherd can't build a house or make clothes

The tailor can't look after cattle or build houses, but makes a lovely cloak

But with specialisation . . .

Three nice houses (all built by the carpenter)

Three fat cows (all tended by the cowherd)

Three well-dressed men (all dressed by the tailor)

and all achieved more quickly than before.

One family might be better at looking after cattle, another better at building shelters, and a third better at growing corn. So gradually the people would concentrate on doing what they were best at, leaving other people to do the things they were not so good at. This is called *specialization*, and has several big advantages over self-sufficiency:

1 Jobs are done better, because the people best at them are doing them.
2 Jobs are done more quickly, because there is less wasted time preparing for different chores and clearing up afterwards.
3 The people doing the jobs get better with practice.

Bartering the surplus

Specialization is the first step towards a more wealthy society, and a community which practised specialization would for the first time have more than enough to keep themselves alive. They would have some things left over – a *surplus*.

Once you have a surplus – things you do not need – you can start *trading*. Trading is simply swapping the things you have but do not need for things other people have that they do not need, but that you would like. In the example above, the cowherd swapped beef for clothes with the tailor. The carpenter swapped housebuilding skills for beef and clothes with the cowherd and tailor. Direct swapping of goods and skills like this is called *bartering*. You have probably *bartered* several things in the past with other people.

I'll give you this knife for your pack of cards

I don't want a knife – I've got three already!

You may have discovered that bartering is not always a very easy way to do business!

It is all right in a very simple society, and can even work between different tribes. A tribe which had no metal could barter furs (for clothing) or animals (for food) with a tribe which made cooking pots and knives but had no animals. And because of specialization, it is likely that a family which spent most of its time working with metal would have little time left over to look after cattle. So there would usually be someone to swap goods with, if you knew where to look. But what if the knife-maker already had plenty of meat? And is a complete cow a fair swap for a small axe?

'Not another cow . . .!'

In fact the problems solve themselves. In any society there is always something you cannot have too many of, because you can always keep the ones you don't need and either use them later, or swap them later for something else. For instance a cow might be worth twenty axes. No one needs twenty axes, but the cowherd can always put nineteen away in his hut, and later on swap them for clothes, cooking pots and so on. So long as axes remain a valuable item, sought after by most people, members of the community can continue to keep them or swap them as required. Instead of bartering goods directly, everyone will end up swapping their goods for axes, and vice versa. Axes will have become the *medium of exchange*, or the tribe's *money*.

What is money?

Obviously the amount an axe is worth will depend on how many axes there are. If there is no shortage of axes, that is if everyone already has one, then axes will not be worth anything. So before anything can become a medium of exchange it must be *scarce*, there must not be too much of it around. Also, if you could imagine a society where everyone had a chain saw, although there might be a shortage of axes, no one would want one because they would be no use. Whatever is used as money must have some *value*, it must be worth having. It also must last a long time, so people can store it and use it for swapping later. Ice-cream would be no good as a medium of exchange because it would melt before you came to swap it for something else! Finally, whatever is used as money must be small and light enough to be able to be carried round and should be able to be split into small pieces for buying little items. A cow is not very suitable!

Anything can be used as money, as long as it is:

> **Scarce**: there is not too much of it around.
> **Valuable**: generally regarded as being worth something.
> **Durable**: lasts a long time without deteriorating

and **Easy to store and carry about**.

It should also be possible to split it into small amounts for buying small items.

Precious metals are ideal, and gold and silver have been used as money for many hundreds of years. Other things have been used as well at various times though, like shells, the feathers of rare birds, and in Europe after the Second World War even cigarettes.

Your work

Write the title 'The growth of money' in your workbook.

1 What would life have been like in a self-sufficient society? What perils might befall a family living in such a society?

2 A primitive society might have increased its wealth by *specialization*. What does this mean, and why would it lead to an increase in wealth?

3 What is a *surplus*?

4 Copy this: 'Anything can be used as money, as long as it is S_____, V_____, D_____and E _____.'

Look at each of the following in turn, and say in what ways it would or would not be able to be used as money (ie Is it scarce? Is it valuable? Is it . . .?

A cow, a knife, diamonds, iron, water.

Now read on . . .

The coming of real money

Originally traders would weigh out small amounts of gold dust when they were buying and selling things, but gradually this system gave way to one using *coins* containing fixed weights of gold and silver. This is the start of money as we know it today.

British £5 note

Once bartering has been replaced by buying and selling for money, it is possible to trade a much wider variety of goods with a much larger group of people. But money brings its own problems. Because it is easy to store and carry about, it is also easy to lose and tempting to steal. And large amounts of gold, too, are heavy. So rather than keep their own gold, people started to leave it in the safekeeping of a bank, obtaining a receipt for it from the banker. Once you have done this it seems a bit silly to go to the bank to get your gold to pay someone else who then goes immediately to the bank and puts the gold back in again. People who trusted each other started paying for goods with the receipts for the gold instead of the gold itself. These receipts were the first *banknotes* and could be exchanged for gold at any time. Our modern notes contain the sentence: 'I promise to pay the bearer on demand the sum of . . . pounds', signed by the Chief Cashier, which is a reminder of those times.

Surprisingly, it is only within the last half century that banks have stopped exchanging notes for gold, and even more recently (in 1947) that our silver coins stopped containing real silver.

However, neither our notes nor our coins have any actual value nowadays in themselves. They are only valuable because people are prepared to swap them for goods. So when the Bank of England burns dirty and worn out notes, they are not actually burning anything valuable, only waste paper, which they replace with brand new notes.

More questions

1 Why is it easier to use money for trading rather than bartering?
2 Imagine you are a banker in the days when people dealt in gold. You take in gold for safekeeping and give receipts out in exchange. Design your receipt. What would it have on it?

Find out

1 Why do 'silver' coins have serrated (jagged, called milling) edges?
3 Nowadays, when you put money in a bank, the bank pays you interest. Why do they pay you for looking after your money?
4 What is a guinea? Does Britain have any gold coins nowadays?

3

The Industrial Revolution

7 Highclose Cottages,
Shepsey.

12th June 1782

Dear Mary,

Thank you for your letter. We are all well here, but are not doing as well as we were with the cloth making. As you know Tom has a loom in the upstairs room to weave the cloth, and our two eldest and myself spin the cotton on our 'spinning jenny' downstairs. 'Jenny' is a short word we use for 'engine'. Thank goodness young David is now four, and able to earn his keep helping young Susan brush the cotton ready for spinning. But Mr. Tomkins, who brings us the cotton each Saturday and collects our finished cloth at the same time has dropped the amount he pays us yet again. He says he has trouble selling the finished cloth in Manchester because the new factories are making it so much more cheaply on their fancy new machines. Tom asked him if we couldn't have one of Arkwright's spinning frames here to replace the old 'jenny', but he just laughed and said even if we could afford it it wouldn't fit into the house, and what's more it needs a horse or a water wheel to power it! I don't know how we're going to manage if this goes on. I suppose you're quite grateful for the cheap cloth because I remember you complaining about the price of clothes at last year's fair, but it means we have to work on Mondays too, which we never used to, only taking Sundays off, if we are to produce enough cloth even to live on.

Tom was saying the other day that he might stop weaving if Fred, who is now nearly fourteen, can manage the loom on his own, and get a job on the new canal they're building near us. He would be called a 'navigator', or 'navvy', and would get paid for his labour - not a lot, but an improvement on what we get now.

Well I must close now. It's getting too dark to see and I don't want to light a candle since I think Tom has almost finished and then we'll all be going to bed.

Love to Bill and the children, Ever yours,

Janet

What was Janet talking about?

First, her letter is completely made up. Everything in it could have been true for a weaver's family in 1782, but she would not have written it. It is most unlikely Janet would have been able to read, and even less likely that she would have been able to write. Neither she nor her children would have gone to school. Even if she had been able to read and write she would probably not have written a letter because her friend Mary would not have been able to pay the postage. In those days the person getting the letter paid for it, and it was not cheap.

Leaving that aside, let us look at what she said. She and her family were *domestic* workers, which means they worked together *at home*. At that time most people did, whether they were weaving cotton or wool, making stockings (common in Leicestershire, Nottinghamshire and Derbyshire), or nails (as in the Midlands). Merchants would take the raw cotton, wool, rods of iron or whatever to people's homes, and collect the finished work. All the family would help. This is an example of *specialization*, with each family doing one job. Not only does each family have special skills though, they also have special *machines* to help them with their work. These machines had developed gradually over hundreds of years and were often provided by the merchants.

Power loom weaving at an early cotton mill

A machine is simply a collection of wheels, axles, levers and pulleys put together to help someone do a particular job. The first machines were concerned with producing food – ploughs, millstones to grind corn, pumps to move water for example. Later machines were invented and built by people in all manner of occupations. Machines continued the gradual progress that specialization had started – the creation of more wealth and more surplus by increasing the work that one person could do.

At the time Janet was writing, this gradual development was being replaced by sudden and enormous changes in the type of machines which were being invented. These changes were to lead to a *revolution* in the way people lived.

Changes in the cotton industry

The change had started in the early 1700s. John Kay invented the 'flying shuttle' in 1738, which enabled a weaver to make wider pieces of cloth more quickly than before. This was followed in 1764 by the invention of the 'spinning jenny' by James Hargreaves which helped the spinner to spin cotton much more quickly than on the old spinning wheels. Janet mentions that she had a spinning jenny, and Tom would also have used a flying shuttle because, like almost all machines built in the hundreds of years leading to this time, the machines were small, and were powered by hand. Because of the huge demand for cloth, though, still better machines were needed.

Janet talks about Arkwright's 'spinning frame'. This was a new machine, much faster than the spinning jenny, but as Mr Tomkins told her, it was too big to fit into the house, and too heavy to be worked by hand. It needed a horse or water wheel to power it.

There was nothing new about either animals being used for power (cattle had pulled ploughs for thousands of years), or water wheels (which had powered mills to make flour for centuries). What was different about the spinning frame was that for the first time the *production of manufactured goods* relied on a machine which needed power. Remember that the houses had no gas or electricity then.

The first factories

So special buildings had to be built to house the new machines. These were the first factories. Originally they were built near fast-flowing rivers and were powered by water wheels, but soon the discovery of steam power meant factories could be built anywhere, and still more powerful machines used.

These early factories were not pleasant places to work in. People had to get used to working set, very long hours, in hot, dangerous conditions. Working long hours was not in itself a problem – under the domestic system people had worked from dawn till dusk – but people found it difficult to get used to having to be at work at a fixed time, and working for six days a week. There were also a great many rules. Some are difficult for us to understand. The rule about not opening windows was because the cotton thread would break if the air got too cool. The fine for being absent was because spinners who were ill were wasting the steam provided for their machine. The pay was very poor.

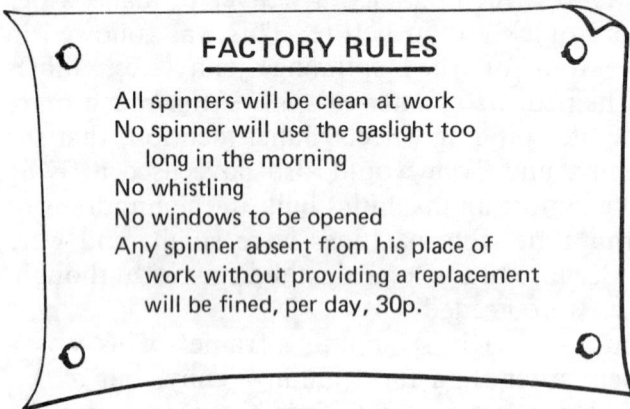

FACTORY RULES

All spinners will be clean at work
No spinner will use the gaslight too
    long in the morning
No whistling
No windows to be opened
Any spinner absent from his place of
    work without providing a replacement
    will be fined, per day, 30p.

We have used the cotton industry as an example of the change from domestic to factory production, and it was the first industry to change. But similar changes in other industries quickly followed. Each invention led to further inventions, as for instance the need for power led to the invention of the steam engine. This led to increased use of coal, which led to hotter fires capable of smelting iron. This brought about changes in the chain-making and other iron-based industries, with resulting increases in the range of metal goods and stronger, faster machines. Furthermore, as more goods, like cotton clothes, are made, so the price drops and the demand for still more goods increases, thus producing a pressure for still faster and bigger machines.

Arkwright's improved spinning machine

A revolution?

We think of a revolution as a change in a country brought about by an armed uprising, like the French or Russian Revolutions. These were *political* revolutions which changed the systems of government in the countries involved. Our Industrial Revolution was rather different. It was a *social* revolution. It too led to great changes in the way people lived and worked, and in the things they could buy, but it was brought about not by fighting, but by inventions. It is called a revolution because it happened so quickly and so dramatically. In 1750 virtually everyone either lived in the country working on the land, or like Janet and Tom as domestic workers. By 1850 three quarters of the population lived in towns and cities, and half the workforce was employed in factories.

And the enormous increase in the country's wealth (the amount of goods and services produced in the country) which industrialization brought during this time, not only vastly increased the amount and type of goods which ordinary people were able to buy, but also directly led to Britain's new position as the wealthiest and most powerful country in the world – ruling three quarters of the world's population, and two thirds of its surface area.

Questions

Write the title 'The Industrial Revolution' and answer the following questions in complete sentences.

1 Why were Janet and Tom called 'domestic workers'?
2 What can you learn from Janet's letter about:
   a) the age at which children were expected to 'pay their way';
   b) the age at which children were considered adult?
3 Why was Tom thinking of working on the canal?
4 What were the changes taking place in cotton making at the time Janet was writing?
5 Why did Janet think her friend would like the changes?
6 Why did the new machines have to be housed in factories?
7 Imagine you are Mary (or her husband Bill) writing back to Janet (or Tom). You work in one of the new factories. Describe your life and how it has changed from what you did before. What is one of your days like?

4

Inventors and inventions

You have seen how the Industrial Revolution came about because of new types of machinery invented at the time. But this is not the whole story. These inventions on their own could not have had such an effect. Like any invention, they had to come at the right time.

Example of an invention at the wrong time

Leonardo da Vinci 'invented' a helicopter in Italy in 1485. That is to say he made drawings of a machine which might just have worked, had he had an engine to power it. But since the discovery of the petrol engine was still four centuries away in the future, his invention came to nothing.

Richard Arkwright's spinning machine came at the right time though. Because of improvements in medicine and agriculture people were healthier and were living longer, and the population was growing. (It doubled between 1750 and 1850, and doubled again between then and 1900.) There was therefore an increasing demand for clothes. And Arkwright's machine used a water wheel (already in existence) to power it. Once such machines are in use, however, new and better ways of powering them (like steam) become inventions at the right time too. And once you have steam, you can then invent machines that would not work without steam power, like locomotives.

All the inventions on these pages happened in Britain during the Industrial Revolution, and all contributed to the growth of factories and modern industries as they are now.

James Watt – steam power

It is said that James Watt got the idea of the steam engine by watching the stream of steam from the spout of a boiling kettle.

This is most unlikely, because a man called **Thomas Newcomen** had already used the principle of steam power in his *beam engine*, which was a pump driven by steam used to clear the water out of mines. What Watt did was to link steam power to a piston and crank, so that steam could turn an axle, and therefore a machine.

The world's first steam engine was built in 1769.

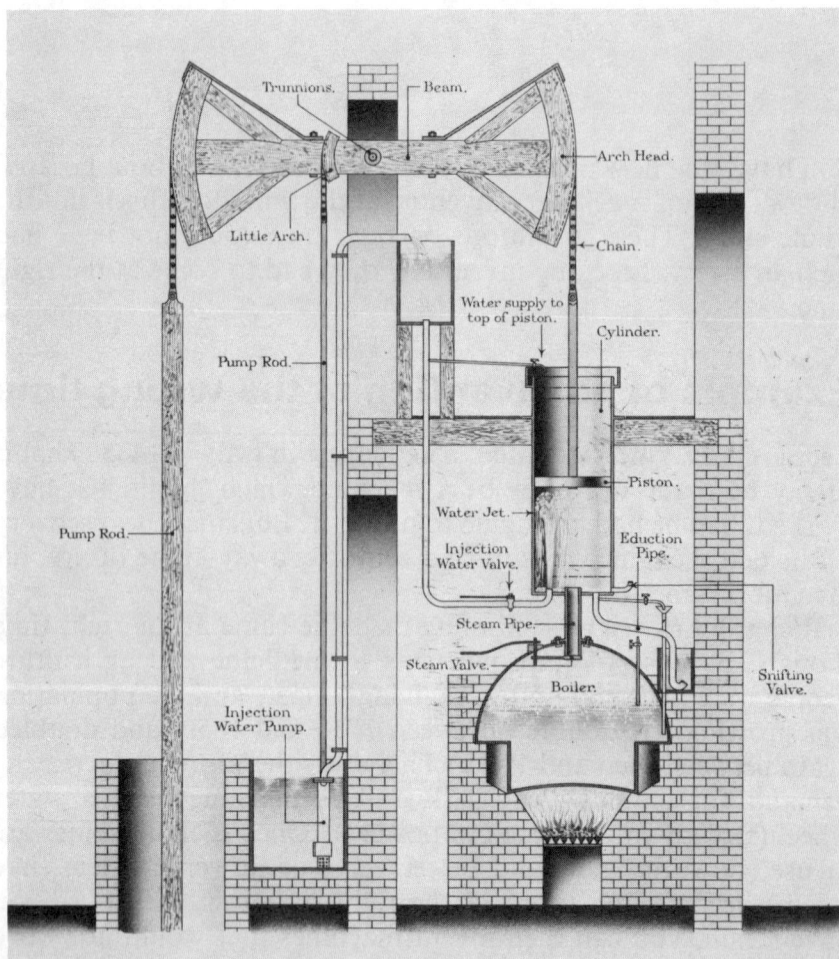

Newcomen's steam pumping engine 1712

This diagram shows a typical atmospheric pumping engine, as made by Newcomen, in section, with the piston in the middle of the downward or working stroke. Steam is generated at atmospheric pressure in the boiler and fills the cylinder during the upward stroke of the piston. The steam valve is then closed and the steam is condensed by a jet of cold water causing a vacuum under the piston. The atmospheric pressure acting on the top of the piston forces it down, hence the name 'atmospheric' engine, and this constitutes the working stroke. The piston is raised again by the overbalancing weight of the pump-rods.

As the Industrial Revolution gathered pace, iron became increasingly important, because of its strength in withstanding the forces in steam driven machines. Once methods of working with iron had improved, all sorts of common articles, from beds to fire grates, could be made with the same techniques.

Abraham Darby

He perfected the process of producing *iron* using coal in 1709. Iron ore is found in many parts of Britain, but to be turned into useful metal, the ore has to be smelted, or heated to a molten state to separate the iron from its ore. This had been done for hundreds of years by using charcoal to heat the ore. Charcoal is obtained by half-burning wood, and smelting iron with charcoal takes a long time and a great deal of wood. Coal, or coke, will produce far more heat than charcoal and can be used on a larger scale. Darby's factory at Coalbrookdale in Shropshire produced large quantities of iron using the new process, building amongst other things the world's first iron bridge there in 1779.

Foundry and mill at Broseley

The Ironbridge, Coalbrookdale, Shropshire

Railways and ships

The first steam locomotive was built by **Richard Trevithick** in 1804. The first railway to carry passengers was built between Stockton and Darlington in 1825, and used **George Stevenson**'s engine 'Locomotion'. The famous 'Rocket' was built in 1830 and powered the first 'proper' railway between Liverpool and Manchester. Railways soon replaced the canals, built over the previous century, as the major way of moving goods around the country from producer to customer. Good transport is essential in an industrial country and the railway network spread quickly. Famous among railway engineers is **Isambard Kingdom Brunel**, who as well as his work on railways built the first steam powered ship to cross the Atlantic in 1845 (the 'Great Britain'). The first iron ship was built in 1818 by the Scot **Thomas Watson**. The iron ships were stronger than wooden ships and had more room inside for cargo, but also needed more power – steam instead of sail. The building of iron ships and the railways greatly increased the demand for iron and later steel during the 19th century.

Agriculture

Changes in food production were vital, leading as they did to the ability to support an increasing population in the industrial towns

Cuguot's locomotive

and cities. **Robert Ransome** invented the metal plough in 1785, and **Jethro Tull** invented the seed drill (for the more efficient sowing of seed) in the 1730s. **Joseph Bryce** built a mechanical reaper (for harvesting crops) in 1799. The biggest advance in agriculture was not an invention at all though.

Jethro Tull's seed drill

It was a series of laws passed in the late 1700s called the 'Enclosure Acts'. These led to farm land being laid out in large fields (instead of the old small strips) enclosed by fences or hedges. Thus the new machinery could be used and previously wasted land brought under cultivation. Fewer people were needed on the land, and many moved to the cities to work in factories.

Coal

Coal has been used as a fuel for thousands of years, but it is most useful in industrial processes in the form of coke. Abraham Darby (see above) discovered how to change coal to coke, and used the process in his ironworks. The subsequent demand for coal and coke to produce iron and steam was satisfied by various developments in mining. In 1816 **Sir Humphrey Davy** invented his famous safety lamp in which the light is surrounded by gauze. The gauze allows air in to keep the lamp alight, but prevents the flame setting fire to the explosive gases found underground. Thomas Newcomen had invented his beam engine to pump water out of mine shafts, thereby allowing deep mining, in 1705, and in 1868 **James Anderton** built a machine to cut the coal off the coal face. It was a revolving cutter very similar to the ones in use today, although whereas his was powered by steam, modern ones use electricity.

Gas

Natural gas has been used for many centuries, but artificial gas (made from coal) was not discovered until the 1600s. It was first used to light a factory in 1798, by **William Murdock**, replacing the feeble and smelly oil lamps, and was brought to the streets of London in 1813. Gas lighting was not very efficient, however, until a German, **Robert von Bunsen**, found a way of mixing air with the gas before it was burnt, in 1855. His invention can still be seen in the bunsen burner. Since then, gas has been used continuously for heating, though not for lighting since the invention of electric power at the turn of the twentieth century. Coal gas was replaced in Britain by natural gas from the North Sea during the 1960s.

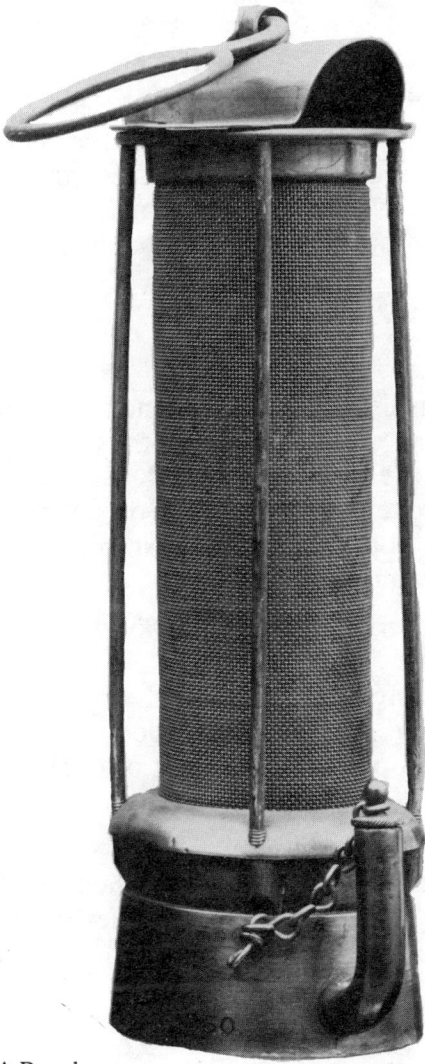

A Davy lamp

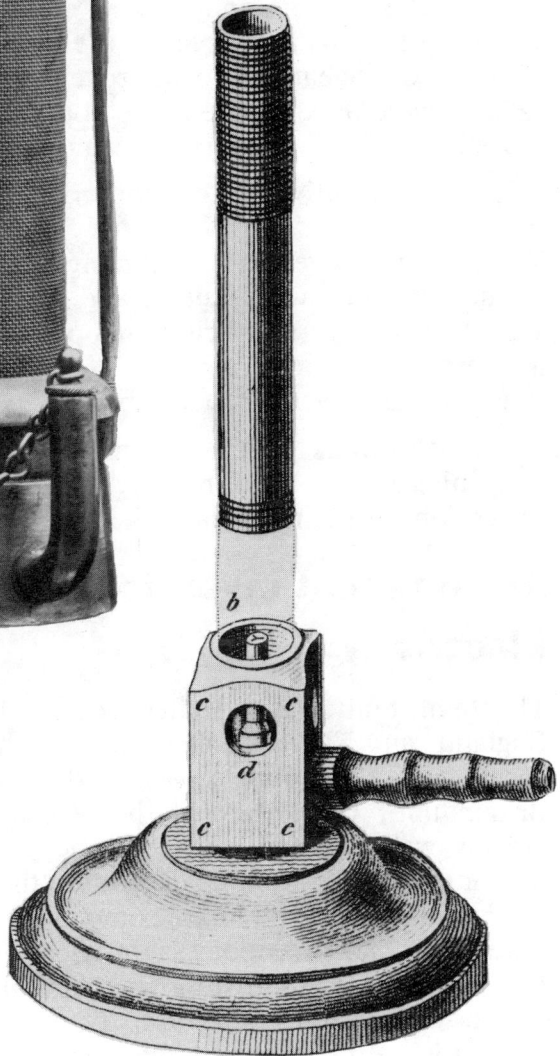

A Bunsen burner

Medicine

Various developments in medicine and public health led to a smaller number of babies dying in infancy, and fewer older children and adults dying from disease. Examples of these are the opening of the London drainage system to sewage in 1815, and the discovery in 1865 of the use of antiseptics to combat infection by **Joseph Lister**.

Summary

All the discoveries and inventions listed above happened between about 1710 and 1850, and together greatly improved the type and quantity of goods produced, or the methods of producing them. This use of inventions to improve the production of goods is called *technology*. People argue about what the most important cause of this huge advance in technology was:

Was it the inventiveness of pioneers like Darby, Arkwright and Brunel?
Was it the improvements in farming and health which caused the population to grow so quickly and demand more goods?
Was it the chance that Britain happens to have a lot of coal and iron ore?
Was it the discovery of steam power?

It is best to think of it as a combination of all these factors all happening together and helping each other – it is a question of 'inventions at the right time'.

More recent inventions
Electricity

The light bulb was invented separately by **Joseph Swan** in England, and **Thomas Edison** in USA in 1879, and the electric generator in 1867, but electricity did not come into general use in Britain until 1900. Part of the reason was that industry was already well supplied with coal and gas. It was only with the building of the London Underground that its advantages became clear, and since then we have come to rely on electricity more and more, with such inventions as the telephone, radio and television. It is worth noting that with the exception of hydro-electricity, all our power stations still use steam to drive their different generators, although the steam is produced in several ways.

Edison's lamp

Oil

Oil has long been used for lighting, and for the lubrication of the new metal machines since 1700. There was a thriving industry extracting oil from oil shale rocks in West Lothian, Scotland, throughout the 19th century. Although petrol had been known about for some time, no use was found for it until the invention of the internal combustion engine in Austria in 1876. A cheaper source of oil (and hence petrol) than oil shale was found with the drilling of the first oil well in Texas in 1870, and these two developments together led to the first motor cars, built by Benz and Daimler in 1885 and 1886. Cars did not become reliable or popular until the 20th century, but were soon to challenge the railways. It was the internal combustion engine too, which led to the invention of the aeroplane by the Wright brothers in 1903, 418 years after da Vinci's 'invention at the wrong time'.

What have you discovered?

Write the title 'Inventions and inventors' in your workbook.

1 Divide your page into columns like this:

Date	Industrial processes	Power sources and machines	Medicine and agriculture	Other devices

Now go through all the inventions and discoveries we have listed in this section between 1700 and 1875 and write them in the appropriate column in *chronological* order (ie put the earliest first). For example Abraham Darby first smelted iron using coke in 1709. So 1709 would go in the first column, and since smelting is an industrial process, you would write 'Darby smelted iron using coke' in the second column.

2 *'The pioneers'*. Write a sentence about each of these particularly significant inventors or pioneers: Abraham Darby, Richard Arkwright, James Watt, Isambard Kingdom Brunel, Richard Trevithick.

3 What does 'technology' mean?

4 Which do you think is the *single most important* invention we have listed? Why this one?

5 Can you find out the dates of these more recent 'firsts': first person in space, first nuclear power station, first jet aircraft, first digital computer.

5

The firm – what it is and does

An industrial firm is like a magician's top hat – certain things go in, something happens to them, and they come out different. The magician waves a magic wand; the firm, unfortunately, has to do rather more! The things that go in are called the *raw materials*. These are the basic things the firm needs to make whatever it produces. The thing that comes out is called the *finished product* – this is what the firm is in business to produce, and what it sells to its customers.

raw materials   finished product

Each finished product has one or more main raw materials, and a lot of more minor ones. For example, the main raw material for most shoes in leather, with various bits of metal, thread and rubber as minor raw materials. The main raw material for cars is steel, and so on.

Questions

Write the title of this section in your book, and answer these questions.

1 What is a raw material?
2 The main raw material for cars is steel. List five other raw materials which also go into producing cars.
3 Take an item of clothing you are wearing which has a label on as your finished product. What have you chosen? Which firm produced this finished product? What were the firm's raw materials (it will say on the label).

Now read on

Every raw material started life originally as a natural product which was either grown or dug out of the ground. One firm after another will have done something to this natural product until it eventually turned into the raw material the final firm needed to transform into its finished product for you, the customer.

The article of clothing you chose in question 3 above could have been made completely from a natural product – wool from sheep, cotton (a plant), or perhaps, if you are very 'dressed up' from silk. It is much more likely, though, that is will have at least some *synthetic*, or manufactured material in it, like *polyester, nylon* or *acrylic*. These raw materials are made originally from oil, and will have been bought by the firm which produced your clothing from an oil or chemical company, perhaps ICI, who in turn produced them from their raw material, oil, a natural product.

Survey

Compare notes with the other members of your class who answered question 3. How many people is that altogether? How many chose clothing made *only* with synthetic products? Now make two lists: one listing all the natural products used as raw materials in the clothing, and the other listing all the synthetics used. What is the most common mixture?

Find out

Why do clothing manufacturers add synthetics to their products? There are three reasons, and you will find a clue to one of them by comparing the washing instructions on all-natural and partly-synthetic clothes.

What goes on inside the magician's hat

So raw materials go in, and a finished product comes out. What goes on inside is a series of *processes*, gradually transforming the raw materials into the finished product.

In science lessons, you may have tried making paper from wood. First you would have chopped the wood into small pieces, then soaked it in water and boiled it until it formed a pulpy mash. Then you would have pressed this pulp, and finally dried it. Because the soaking and boiling of wood takes a long time, you might well have started with straw, but the principle is the same. You would have taken the wood through four different processes:

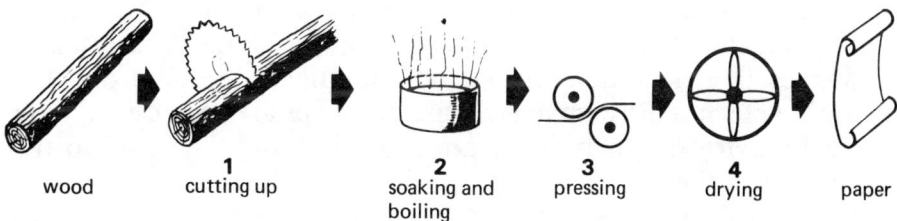

wood — **1** cutting up — **2** soaking and boiling — **3** pressing — **4** drying — paper

Your raw material was wood, your finished product paper. Each process requires different machinery, and each process brings the wood gradually nearer to being paper.

A *firm* manufacturing paper does much the same thing, only on a much larger scale. Also, a paper manufacturer will use various other raw materials as well as wood, like chemicals to speed up the pulp making, and bleach to make the paper white.

Notice that just as each process requires its own machinery, so it usually has its own *workers*. People generally work on one process, dealing with the raw material in the state it comes to them, and then passing it on to other workers with other machines in its new state, for the next process. This principle can be seen in its most extreme form on a *production line*, where the product being made moves on a *conveyor belt* from one process (group of workers and machines) to the next.

Fact . . . The longest indoor conveyor belt in Britain is in the British Leyland car factory at Longbridge, in Birmingham.

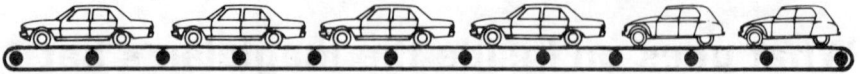

Anything else?

Yes. The firm needs raw materials to turn into finished products. It does this by subjecting the raw materials to a series of processes, each of which brings them closer to being the finished product – the manufactured article.

But the firm needs four other things before the processes can work. Two of them we have already mentioned: the firm needs workers, and it needs machines. Workers are called *labour*, and by this we mean *everyone* who works in the firm, from the person who sweeps the floor, to the Managing Director.

Machines are part of the firm's *capital*. This is all the fixed items which the firm needs, and which stay with the firm. Capital includes the machines, the factory buildings, the land and the firm's vehicles. Raw materials are *not* capital, because they do not stay with the firm. They are processed and then sold to the firm's customers.

The third thing the firm needs is *energy* to work the machines and heat and light the factory. This energy is usually electricity, coal, oil or gas, or a combination of these. Energy, as anyone will tell you, is expensive, and many industrial processes (like those involved in making paper) use a great deal of it.

Finally, the firm needs someone, or a group of people, with the brains and the initiative to start the firm up, to expand it, to develop it, and to keep it running. This combination of brains and initiative is called *enterprise*.

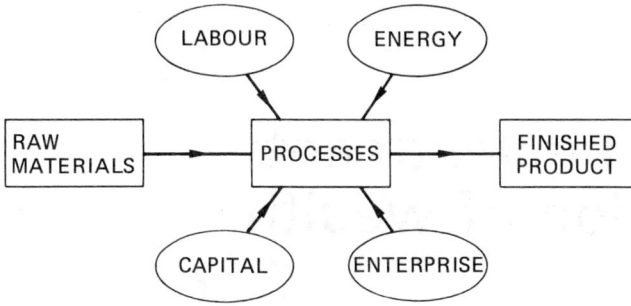

More questions

Remember to write neatly, and in complete sentences – could someone who hasn't read this book understand your answers?

THINK

of a firm which makes leather shoes.
1 What is the firm's *finished product*?
2 What is the firm's main *raw material*?
3 What are the main *processes* the raw material will go through before it becomes the finished product? Draw a diagram showing the processes (like we did for the manufacture of paper). Say what the raw material will have been changed to after each process.
4 What other raw materials will the firm use, apart from the one you named in question 2 above?
5 What other *four* things, apart from raw materials, will the firm need in order to manufacture its finished product? Write each one in capital letters, and then explain what it is, and why it is needed.
6 Say whether each of the following is *capital, raw material,* or *energy*:
   The oil BP turns into petrol.
   The oil British Leyland uses to heat its factories.
   A window cleaner's chamois (shammy) leather.
7 And finally, explain the difference between a *firm*, and a *factory*.

6

Profit and investment – the creation of wealth

Question: 'What is the wealth of a country?'
Answer: 'The amount of goods and services that country produces.'

We are not concerned in this book with how the wealth is divided up – who gets how much of the national 'cake' – although dividing the cake *fairly* (which does not always mean equally) is a very important job of the government.

My piece

Your piece!

We are instead concerned with the clear fact that the bigger the cake is, the more there is to divide. The amount of goods we produce in Britain is not fixed, it can increase or decrease, and it is obviously in everyone's interest to try and make it increase. We have already seen that the wealth of Britain increased enormously during the Industrial Revolution due to the *growth of industries* brought about by *technological advance*. The new inventions at the time led to far more being produced. So technological advance is one method of increasing wealth.

Technological advance

Let us look at this in the context of an individual firm such as we examined in the last chapter. Raw materials are *processed* into finished products, and the processes each use their own machinery. Replacing old machines with new, more efficient ones, and trying to develop new and better products are two ways a firm can increase its output – the amount of goods it produces. When a firm spends money doing either of these things it is called *investment*. Investment might take the form of simply buying new machinery. Or a large firm might employ scientists whose job is *research and development* (sometimes called R & D); that is trying to discover new and better processes or products. One of the reasons Britain's industrial growth has lagged behind that of countries like Germany and Japan since the Second World War is because those countries needed new machines to replace industries completely destroyed in the war, whereas many firms in Britain continued to use machines dating back, in some cases, well into the 19th century.

Investment costs money.

Where the money comes from

A firm's money comes from selling the goods it produces. This money has to pay for the raw materials, the labour force, the energy costs and any payments for capital items, like rent and rates for buildings, repair bills, replacement of worn out vehicles and machines, and so on. Any money left over is the firm's *profit*. If there is nothing left over, no profit, the firm will eventually go *bankrupt*, will be unable to pay its bills, and will have to close down and sack all its workers.

If there is some profit, the firm will be able to spend some of it in *investment* in new machines, research, a bigger factory, or developing new products. It is quite likely, though, that a firm will want to spend more on investment than it makes in profits, so it will need to raise some extra money. It can do this in two ways:

1 Borrowing

A firm can borrow money from a bank, or from anyone else who will lend it. The lender will expect to be paid back, of course, and will expect to get *interest* on the money. These payments will come from a firm's future profits in years to come. So a firm has to be making a profit, or has to look as if it might, before anyone will lend it money.

2 Selling shares

A firm might raise money by selling shares in itself to members of the public. Anyone buying a 'share' in the firm will give money to the firm (for investment) and in exchange will become a part-owner of the firm, or *shareholder*. Each year shareholders receive part of the firm's profits, called a *dividend*. This is their return for giving the firm their money, so obviously the bigger the dividend they expect, the more likely they will be to buy a share in the firm. Shareholders are never repaid – they give money to the firm not lend it – but if they want to stop being owners, they can sell their share to someone else. The *Stock Exchange* is the place where people sell shares to each other, and big companies have literally millions of shares, some of which change hands every day. The money people give to firms in this way is called *risk capital*: 'capital' because it goes towards capital spending, and 'risk' because the shareholders are risking their money and will lose some or all of it if the firm does badly.

There is a limit to the amount a firm can borrow since the money has to be paid back, often fairly quickly, so practically all firms, at one time or another, will have raised money by selling shares to the public. In 1981, British Petroleum (BP) raised over six hundred million pounds for new investment in this way.

A firm whose owners are members of the public is called a *public company*, although many shares nowadays are owned by pension funds, investment trusts or trade unions.

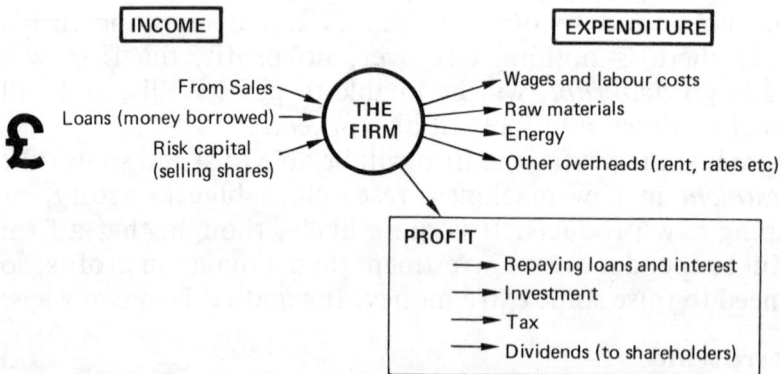

| INCOME | | EXPENDITURE |

£

From Sales
Loans (money borrowed) → THE FIRM
Risk capital (selling shares)

Wages and labour costs
Raw materials
Energy
Other overheads (rent, rates etc)

PROFIT
→ Repaying loans and interest
→ Investment
→ Tax
→ Dividends (to shareholders)

A firm that does not make any profit will
not be able to borrow money or repay existing loans,
not be able to invest in new machinery, and so increase the amount of goods it produces,

not be able to pay dividends to shareholders, and so will be unable to raise new money for investment.

Other ways to increase wealth

Investment is very important, but it is not the only way to increase either production or profits. Profits will increase if expenditure goes down, like by the firm using less electricity. Or if the firm sells more, perhaps by more advertising or better marketing, its profits will go up. Note that putting up prices does not automatically mean a firm will make more money. Often it simply means the firm will sell fewer goods, and make even less profit. Sir Jack Cohen, who founded Tesco, once said: 'Pile it high, and sell it cheap!', meaning that if a firm sells things cheaply it will sell lots of them, and hence make a lot of profit. It certainly worked for him! It is a complicated job for a firm to fix its prices so they are high enough to make a profit, but low enough to sell the goods.

And if a firm can produce the same number of goods more cheaply than before, or more goods for the same cost, its profits will increase. This would happen if the firm persuaded its workers to work harder or more quickly, as well as by investment in more efficient machinery.

The amount of goods produced by a firm for a given number of workers is called its *productivity*. If productivity goes *up*, the firm will be making more goods than before with the same number of workers. If productivity goes *down*, the firm will be making less. Productivity can be increased by investment in more efficient machinery, or by improving the quality and work of the workforce, or by both.

The Gazelle Motor Company makes 10 cars per year for each worker.

The Elland Motor Company makes 20 cars per year for each worker.

Elland cars will be cheaper and the Elland Company will make more profit because each workers wages are shared among 20 cars instead of 10.

Cutting down expenses = more profit
Selling more goods = more profit
Increasing productivity = more profit
More profit = more investment = more goods produced = increased wealth

All these concerns – how much to charge, how to cut down expenses, how to sell more goods, whether and how to invest, how to improve the product, how to increase productivity – are the job of the *management* of the firm.

Questions

Write the title of this section in your workbook.
1 Copy out the diagram showing a firm's 'income' and 'expenditure'.
2 Say what each of these words means (read back over the section to help you get the meanings accurate): profit; investment; productivity; risk capital
3 Rewrite this sentence *without* using the word 'productivity': 'The productivity of the Japanese ship-building industry is greater than the productivity of the British ship-building industry.'
4 What are the main ways in which a company can raise money for investment if its profits are not large enough to pay for the investment directly?
5 If you were the manager of a firm, and you wanted to increase your firm's profits, what different ways could you go about doing this?
6 Some goods are very *sensitive* to price changes – ie if a firm puts its price up that firm will immediately lose a lot of their sales. Others are *resistant* to price change. Say whether you think each of the following is sensitive or resistant to price change, and why: petrol; gas; cigarettes; sheepskin coats; ball-point pens.

Find out

Most newspapers give lists of the share prices of at least our major companies. Can you find out what is the current price of shares in BP and Marks and Spencer? If you or your teacher has a copy of a paper giving a large list of share prices (like the *Daily Telegraph* or the *Scotsman*) your teacher will be able to help you work out what dividend shareholders in these companies got for each share last year. Can you find the share prices of any of your local companies?

7

Different types of industry

There are many thousands of different firms in Britain. Some employ tens of thousands of workers, others employ only one or two. Some are household names, others have not been heard of outside their immediate town, or even road. Some big firms you will not have heard of because they only sell goods to other firms, and not to the public. Some firms use a great deal of machinery, other very little. Some firms only make goods, others only sell them; a few do both. Because of all these differences it is useful to try and sort firms out, or classify them, by looking at the types of things they do.

ARC's Batts Combe Quarry, Frome, Somerset

Primary industry

All raw materials started out initially as natural products which were grown or dug out of the land or sea. The firms which grow them or dig them out are called *primary* firms, and make up our primary industry. Primary means the first stage (like primary schools are the first stage in education), and primary industry deals with the *first stage* in the production of goods.

Examples of primary industry are *farming*, *fishing*, *forestry*, *mining*, *quarrying* and the *oil industry*. In all of these a natural product is either grown, harvested, or extracted from the earth or sea. Among our biggest primary firms are the Forestry Commission, the National Coal Board and British Petroleum (BP), but there are also many smaller firms involved in this work. Many of them you will never hear of because they only sell raw materials, like limestone, leather, silicon and aluminium to other firms for these firms to process and so turn into manufactured goods.

Note: the difference between mining and quarrying is that in a mine the product (coal, iron ore or whatever) has to be dug from under the ground, whereas in a quarry it is available at the surface, for example on the side of a hill.

Manufacturing industry

Manufacturing industry is the next stage in production, and is sometimes called *secondary industry*. The types of firms we looked at in Chapter 5 were manufacturing firms. A manufacturing firm takes a number of raw materials (often from primary firms) and turns them through processing into finished products. Whereas primary industry can be found at mines, farms and oil wells, manufacturing industry takes place in factories.

Virtually all the products we buy in shops, with the exception of fresh food, were produced by manufacturing firms. Major British manufacturers include British Leyland, Tube Investments (TI – who make Creda, Russell Hobbs and Raleigh products), Guest Keen and Nettlefolds (GKN – who make many car components among other things), Lucas and British Aerospace. Major foreign manufacturers of whom you may have heard include Datsun, IBM (who make computers) and Sony.

Service industry

A great many firms do not actually make anything. They either transport people or goods, sell goods, provide financial services like banking and insurance, provide education and health services, or provide personal services like catering, hairdressing, window cleaning and the like. All these firms are classed as *service industry*, because they provide services to other firms or members of the public. In addition the government and local authorities provide services and are therefore included in Service Industry, although they are not really firms. Because these firms provide the final, or third stage in the production of goods, the stage of bringing goods from the factory to the shop and customer, they are sometimes called *tertiary* industry.

Where people work

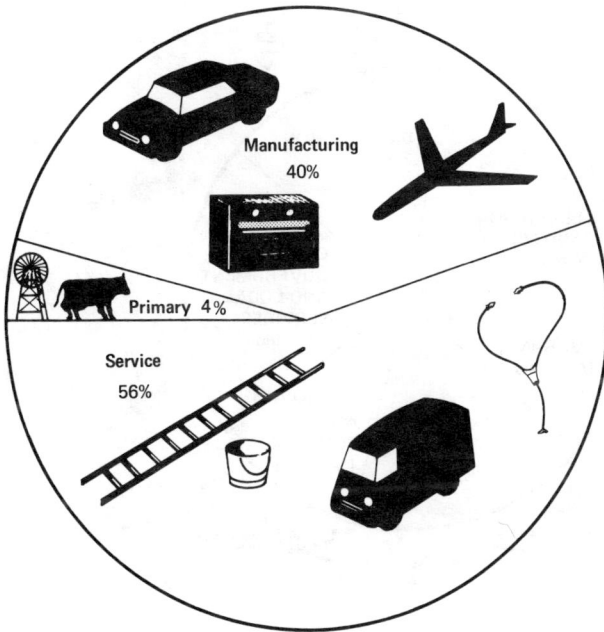

Manufacturing
40%

Primary 4%

Service
56%

This is very different from the picture at the beginning of the century, when 10% of the workforce worked in mining (a primary industry) alone. At that time far more people than today worked in manufacturing industry as well. The trend has been for more and more of the population to be employed in service industry as the years have gone by, and comparatively fewer in primary and manfacturing industry. This trend is still continuing.

Why so many in service industries?

This is typical of the richer industrial countries. As industry becomes more efficient and productive, fewer people are required to produce the same amount of goods. Because less people are employed, but are producing just as much, their pay goes up and they can afford to spend it on services as well as goods. This increased demand for services requires more people to provide them – the people who are no longer needed in manufacturing. Remember that the *wealth* of a country includes the value of the services it provides as well as the goods it makes. However without manufacturing industry to produce the wealth initially in the form of goods, there would be no money to provide any services at all.

Because so many people work in service industries, we will break this down into different sections:

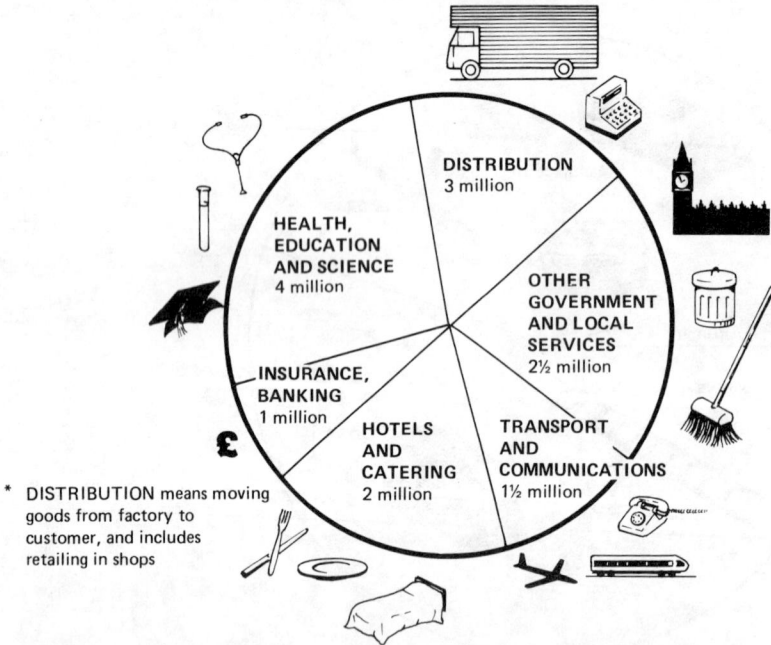

DISTRIBUTION
3 million

HEALTH, EDUCATION AND SCIENCE
4 million

OTHER GOVERNMENT AND LOCAL SERVICES
2½ million

INSURANCE, BANKING
1 million

HOTELS AND CATERING
2 million

TRANSPORT AND COMMUNICATIONS
1½ million

* DISTRIBUTION means moving goods from factory to customer, and includes retailing in shops

You will be able to count up and see that fourteen million people work in service industries, out of a total workforce of about twenty-five million people. There are fifty-six million people living in Britain, the thirty-one million who are not in employment being roughly equally divided between children at school and below age five, mothers who are at home bringing up children, and people who have retired from work due to age or ill health.

40

Types of employers

Nearly seven people out of every ten work for a private firm. This means a firm which has shareholders who have either invested their money in the firm, or have bought shares in the firm off previous shareholders. Many of the shareholders, who actually own the firm, are members of the public, but some shares are owned by trade unions, pension funds or the government. Firms whose shares can be bought and sold at The Stock Exchange by members of the public are called *public companies*.

Some firms are completely owned by the government, and have no other shareholders. These are called *nationalized industries* in the case of firms which were once private but which for one reason or another the government has now taken over, or *public corporations* in the case of the few organizations the government started from scratch. Some firms were *nationalized* (bought by the government) because they could no longer afford the massive sums needed to invest in modern machinery without government help. Examples are British Rail and British Airways. Others, like British Leyland, were nationalized because they went bankrupt and the government did not want them to close down and therefore cause a lot of unemployment. A third group of firms were nationalized because the government at the time thought they ought to be owned by everyone (ie the government) rather than by individual people. British Steel falls into this group. Examples of Public Corporations are The Post Office, British Telecom, and the BBC. One worker in twelve is employed by a nationalized industry or public corporation.

In addition, 20% of the workforce (one worker in five) is employed by the government directly (the civil service), or by the local authorities, the health boards or the armed forces.

And one worker in fourteen is *self-employed* – that is they work on their own account, perhaps as a window cleaner or builder, and are not employed by anyone.

Private sector 72%		Public sector 28%	
Private firms (including public companies) 65%	Self-employed 7%	Nationalised industries 8%	Govt,local authorities etc 20%

Questions

Write the title 'Types of industry' in your workbook.
1 Write down *definitions* (what they mean) of primary, manufacturing and service industry.
2 Draw three columns across your page, headed 'primary', 'manufacturing' and 'service'.
   a) Put each of these activities in the correct column: herring fishing, shoe-making, coal mining, window cleaning, making ball-point pens, drilling for oil, teaching, making cars and nursing.
   b) And now do the same for each of these firms or organizations: Shell, Pye, the Forestry Commission, the National Health Service, Ford, Marks and Spencer, British Airways.
3 Is the number of people employed in service industries getting bigger or smaller? Why?
4 Look at the five headings (excluding the government) which we gave for service industry. Can you name two firms or other organizations under each heading?
5 Are more people in Britain employed, or not employed? What are those who are not employed doing?
6 Draw a pie chart showing the proportions of the workforce employed by private firms, self-employed, working for nationalized industries and public corporations, and working for the government and local authorities.

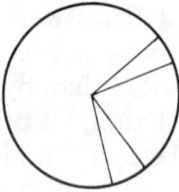

8

The structure of a firm

Jane to the class teacher: 'How come the Headteacher gets paid more than you, just for sitting in an office all day when you've got the job of teaching us?'

Try asking your teacher this (unless he or she *is* the Headteacher) and see what answer you get! Remember it is considered *very bad manners* to ask anyone *how much* they earn, unless they are a very close friend of yours.

One of the answers your teacher will give, assuming he or she does not say, 'I really can't imagine!' is that the Headteacher is in charge of the whole school, and is responsible for everything that goes on in it. He or she started as an ordinary teacher and has been *promoted* to a higher post because of special skills and abilities. By giving the Head more money, the school is not only recognizing this responsibility, but is encouraging teachers to want to get promoted, thereby trying to make sure that the best people available get the highest jobs.

But there is not just a Head and teachers in a school. You probably know that some of your teachers have been promoted to other jobs, each having special responsibilities. These might include Heads of Department, responsible for all the teaching in a particular subject; Heads of Year or House responsible for the welfare of the pupils in a particular year group or House; there might be an Assistant or Deputy Head, responsible for directly helping the Head in his or her job.

Task

Identify the *promoted* teachers in your school, and say what each is responsible for. Can you arrange them in order from the Head down? Some will be equal – you could place them on the same line below the person above them.

Unless your school is very small, it could not run effectively without some of the teachers being given these special responsibilities.

The firm

The same happens in a firm. Some people are given special responsibilities, to help the firm run efficiently. In any group of workers, one will be put in charge to see the others work properly. This person will be called a *supervisor* or *charge-hand*. If there are a number of different groups of workers, then one person will be in charge of all of them, to help the supervisors, and to deal with any problems the supervisor cannot manage. This person is often called the *foreman*. He or she is particularly important being the link between the factory 'floor', and the more senior *managers* who generally work from offices.

The foreman will report to the *Production manager*, who is in charge of all the firm's production. He or she will do far more than just see that everyone works properly though. It is also his or her job to see that the machines work as much of the time as possible, that materials are in the right places at the right times, that orders are made up when required, and to tell other managers what it is possible to produce, and when.

Other managers

There will probably be a *Sales manager* as well. He or she is responsible for selling what the firm makes, and may have responsibility for a team of sales staff. The *Personnel manager* is responsible for the recruitment and welfare of the people employed by the firm and will deal with problems about pay and conditions, and with holiday arrangements. In a firm with a large office staff, there may be an *Office manager* in charge of all the secretarial and office staff. There will probably also be a *Company secretary* or *Accountant* to deal with the financial and legal side of the business.

In a large firm

These managers will probably have assistants to help them, and there may be other managers dealing with particular aspects of a firm, like a *Customer services manager* to deal with any queries from customers. And there might be a *Research and development manager* to look at ways of improving the firm's products and methods.

The production manager in particular might have other managers working for him or her taking responsibility for different aspects of production. These could include some or all of the following.

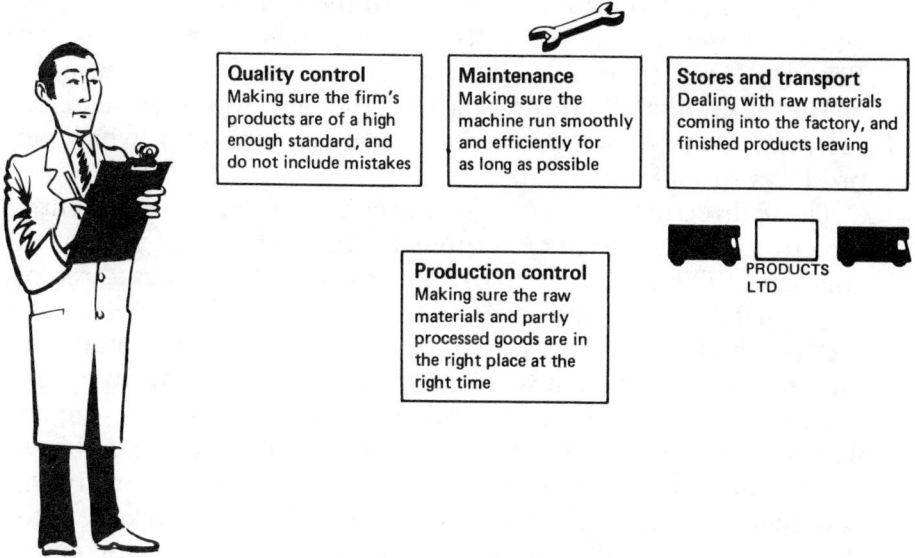

Quality control
Making sure the firm's products are of a high enough standard, and do not include mistakes

Maintenance
Making sure the machine run smoothly and efficiently for as long as possible

Stores and transport
Dealing with raw materials coming into the factory, and finished products leaving

Production control
Making sure the raw materials and partly processed goods are in the right place at the right time

PRODUCTS
LTD

The employer

There will be one person in overall charge of the firm. He or she might be called the *General manager,* or if the owner of the firm, the Proprietor or, if a woman, the Proprietress. This person is like the Headteacher in your school.

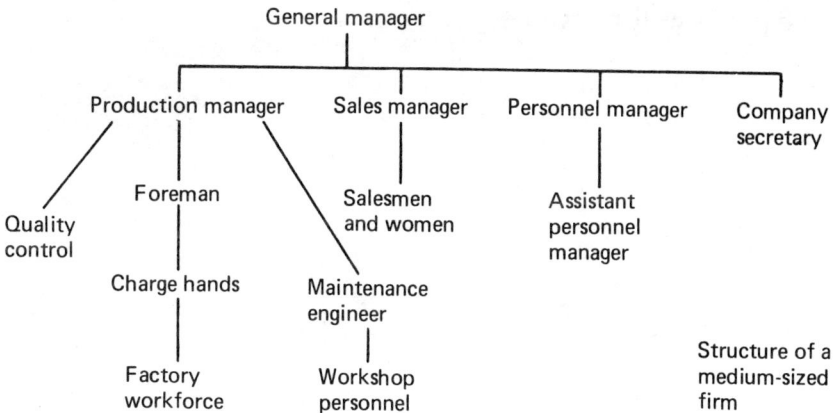

General manager

Production manager — Sales manager — Personnel manager — Company secretary

Quality control

Foreman

Salesmen and women

Assistant personnel manager

Charge hands

Maintenance engineer

Factory workforce

Workshop personnel

Structure of a medium-sized firm

Directors

A company is owned by the shareholders. They appoint a group of people, some of whom are themselves shareholders, some of whom work for the company, to run the company on their behalf. The shareholders elect these people by voting for them at the company's *Annual General Meeting* (or AGM). The people elected form the *Board of Directors* of the company. One of them will be chosen by the others to be *Chairman* of the Board. The Board of Directors meets periodically to make major decisions about the company's future, like whether and where to build new factories, what new machinery to invest in, and what new products to make.

Those directors who work for the company are called executive directors, and will each be responsible for a particular area of the company. There will be a Production director, Sales director, Personnel director, and so on.

A company might run several different firms with a number of factories, each of which will have its own structure of managers. We mentioned Tube Investments in the last chapter, a company which owns several firms, among them both Creda and Russell Hobbs. Or it might be a small company of just one firm. In this case the managers and directors might be the same people – the Production director would also be the Production manager. However large or small the company, one of the directors – the *Managing director* – will be in overall charge of the day to day running of the company.

Special note to all

Most managers *are* in fact men, but some are women, and there is no reason at all why any of the jobs we have mentioned cannot be done equally well by women as by men.

Questions

Write the title 'The structure of a firm' in your workbook, and answer these questions.

1 Copy out the diagram of 'the structure of a medium-sized firm'. Make a list of the people you have included in the diagram, and by each one give a short description of their job.

2 What jobs do you think the Production manager of a large firm might have done in the past before being promoted?

3 Imagine you are the Personnel manager of a firm and have to give instructions to a new young recruit on how to treat the foreman. What would you say?

4 Which managers will have most contact, and why, with:
   a) the factory workforce
   b) the general public?

5 If you were an electrical apprentice working in the maintenance section of a factory, what would your job involve? Who would probably be directly in charge of you? Who would he be responsible to?

Further work

Your teacher many be able to arrange for you to visit a local factory and ask them about their structure of jobs. What managers do they have? Is there a Board of Directors, and if so, where? Who is responsible for quality control? And for new recruits?

9

Methods of production

The envelope exercise

The class should be arranged in groups of four people. Each group gets: a supply of paper, a ruler, a pen or pencil, a pair of scissors and some glue. The task is to make as many envelopes as possible in fifteen minutes which conform to the pattern shown below. The pattern is not drawn to full size.

Pattern

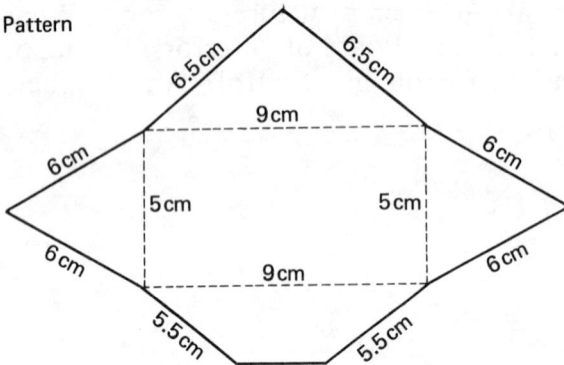

Finished product

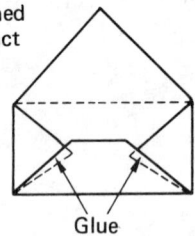

Glue

Before you start, your teacher should let each group draw one correct pattern to full size.

GO

STOP

Your teacher will now act as *quality controller* and decide how many of the envelopes each group made are up to the standard required. Which group won?

How you did it

You could have used a number of different methods:

Individual production: Each of you might have drawn a pattern, cut out the shape and then glued it. If you did this each of you would be able to identify some of your group's envelopes as 'my' envelopes. This is the *craftsman* approach, and would have been rather slow, particularly since you probably wasted a lot of time waiting for the scissors, ruler or glue.

Specialization: You might have *specialized*, dividing your labour into the different processes. One person would have done all the drawing, another the cutting, a third the folding, and the fourth the glueing. This is much quicker than individual production, and you would have got even faster as you each got more practised at your particular process.

Mass production: The fastest group will almost certainly have used some mass-production. This is when you produce a lot of parts for your finished product at the same time on their own, rather than making one, passing it on to the next process, then making another, and so on. The easiest way of bringing mass-production into the envelope making would have been to use one envelope pattern as a *template*, then putting several sheets of paper underneath it and cutting through them together. This is not only much quicker than cutting them out individually, it also removes one process altogether – that of drawing the pattern on to the paper.

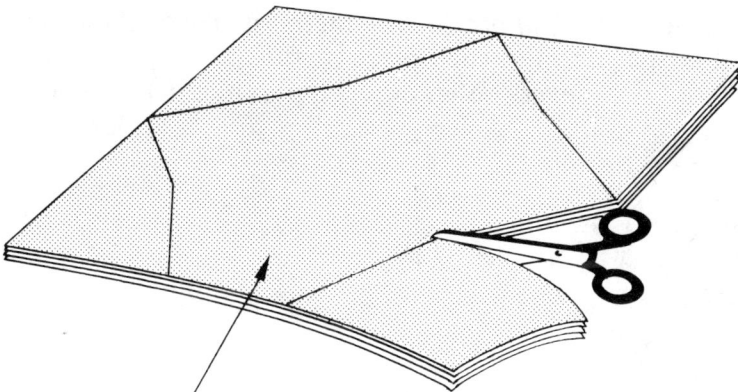

Template

Production control

Whichever way you made your envelopes, you will have found there were times when you could not work because you either had no materials ready for your process, or no equipment available to work with. In a factory it is the job of the *production controller* to arrange things so that this happens as little as possible. One way is to provide more equipment – would an extra pair of scissors have helped you? Another way is to arrange the work-force so that more people work on one process than another (ie two people folding but only one cutting out, because the folding takes longer).

Another way is to introduce some *job-rotation*. This means that when the cutter-out has finished a batch of patterns, he or she then joins the folders to help fold them. Job-rotation is not possible when one job requires particular skills the other workers do not have. When people will not do another job because it is not the job they are employed to do, it is called *demarcation*. A demarcation dispute would arise if the production controller told a person to help with someone else's job and he or she refused because it was 'not my job'. Some demarcation is necessary if special skills are involved, particularly when aspects of safety are concerned, but otherwise demarcation can lead to inefficiency and lower productivity.

When different production methods are used

A craftsman who takes a piece of wood and turns it into a chair or table is using *individual production* methods. He or she will be very skilled at the job, and each piece of furniture made will be unique (there will never be another quite like it). Each of

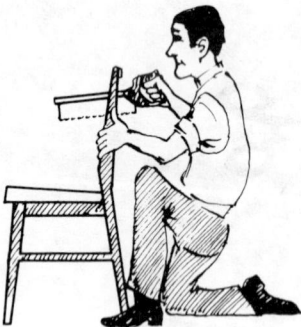
The craftsman

their finished products will have taken a long time to make, and will be very expensive. This method of production is consequently very rare, especially in factories.

Most factories use *specialization*, dividing their labour by process, so that each worker becomes practised at working the machinery used in his or her particular process. The worker does not need to be skilled at every process, therefore, like the crafts-man is. One person will make the table legs, another the tops, and so on, with a final group of *assembly workers* putting the table together. Because each piece of the finished table is made on the same machine, and has to match the other pieces, all the finished tables will be virtually identical.

Mass production simply means making a lot of one piece of the finished product together, and separately from the rest of the pieces. Some goods can be made entirely by continuous mass pro-duction, since they contain only one part. Examples are razor blades, buttons, or nails.

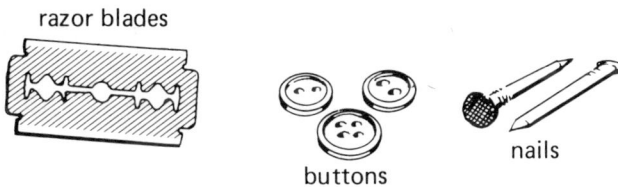

razor blades

buttons

nails

| locks | bars of chocolate | ball-point pens |

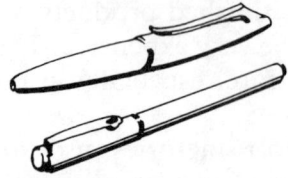

Other goods have all their parts made by continuous mass production, and are then assembled, like locks, bars of chocolate and ball-point pens.

Batch production is used when a firm wishes to make only a certain number of finished products, instead of having a continuous stream. Aeroplanes, books, and often furniture are examples of this type of product.

Flow production is used when raw materials are gradually treated as they pass through the factory's processes, turning eventually into the finished product, but where they are not an assembly of different mass produced pieces. Petrol, beer and sugar are produced by flow production.

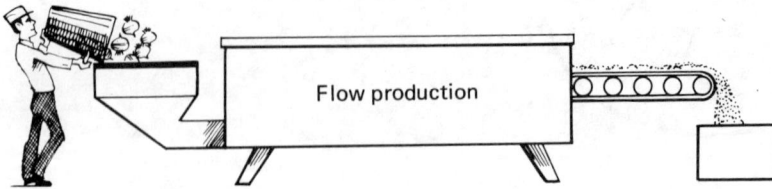

Flow production

Finally, *one-off production* is used where a firm is producing only one very large or specialized item, such as a ship, a special machine, or a satellite.

Questions

Write the title of this section in your workbook, and answer the following questions. Do not forget to use complete sentences.

1 Thinking of your envelope exercise:
    a) How did you arrange your production? Who did what?
    b) Did you use specialization? In what way?
    c) Did you use mass production? How? If you did not, how could you have done?
    d) What is a production controller's job? Who acted as production controller in your group? (Perhaps you did it together.)
    e) What is job rotation? Did you use any job rotation?
2 What is a 'demarcation dispute'?
3 What does an 'assembly worker' do?
4 Describe what is meant by each of: mass production, batch production, flow production, one off production, and individual production (craftsman method).
5 Give two examples, other than the ones we gave, of products which might be made by each of these methods.
6 You are looking at three tables. How could you tell whether they had been made individually by a craftsworker, or mass produced in a factory?

Note to furniture detectives. Some furniture nowadays is mass produced and assembled, and then has individual carving put on bits of it to make it look craftsman produced without the expense. Most modern furniture is made of *chipboard*, at least the flat bits of it, with a very thin layer (called a *veneer*) of real wood on top. In some cases even the veneer is not wood, but plastic made to look like wood.

10

A nation of shopkeepers

Britain is one of the most efficient food-producing countries in the world. Canada is forty times as big, yet our farmers produce more food than the Canadian farmers. We produce more food than Australia and New Zealand combined. Only 1% of Britain's workforce works on the land, and they grow and rear enough food for half our population. But because our population is so large we still have to buy enormous amounts of food from other countries. In fact we are the world's largest *importers* of food.

Imports are things we buy from other countries
Exports are things we sell to other countries. 'Ex' means 'out of' (like in exit), so exports are things which go *out of* our sea and airports.

Because of this, we depend very heavily on selling things to other countries, in order to give us foreign money, or currency, to buy food from abroad. Trading with other countries is essential to us. Of course, we do not only buy food; there are other things we need that we cannot produce ourselves, and things which other countries can make more cheaply. Most importantly, we need to import many *raw materials* to keep our industry going, like copper, iron ore, timber and zinc, from which we produce manufactured goods.

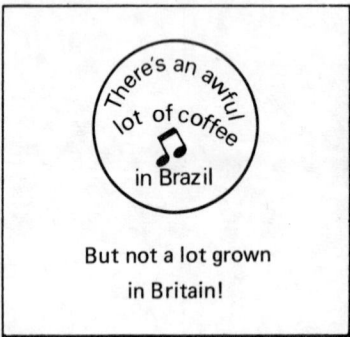

There's an awful lot of coffee ♪ in Brazil

But not a lot grown in Britain!

Britain's Fort Knox

The Bank of England has a large store, or reserve, of gold and foreign currency which importers can exchange for their pound notes in order to pay other countries for their food, raw materials and other goods. This would very soon all be used up though (probably in a few weeks) if other countries were not paying us gold or foreign currency for things they wanted to buy off us. Obviously the value of our *exports* must be sufficient to pay for our *imports*. If it is not enough, and this happens quite often, the government can make exports cheaper, so we sell more, by lowering the value of the pound. This means that foreign countries can get more pounds than before for the same number of dollars, francs or yen. While the result is that we sell more abroad, it also means that *all* our imports, including food and raw materials, became more expensive. Conversely, if the value of our exports is *more* than our imports, the government can afford to raise the value of the pound, which will make our imports cheaper.

This is why the value of the pound is important to all of us, and is given each day at the end of the national news, and in most newspapers.

Since we *have* to import food and raw materials, we *must* sell enough abroad to pay for them.

If we buy things from foreign countries that we could buy from British firms, we have to sell all the more abroad to pay for them – so we should always look at British made goods first when we are planning to buy something, and only choose foreign goods if the British ones are not suitable. To help us do this, everything made abroad must be marked as 'foreign' or have its country of origin given, as in 'Made in France'.

Buy British!

What we have to sell

On the face of it, we do not have a lot to sell. Some oil, and a bit of coal, and that's about it. So we make our money by selling *manufactured goods*, like cars, aeroplanes, ships, chemicals and computers; *services* (called *invisibles*), like insurance, banking and tourism; and *technical expertise* in fields like building, nuclear technology, education and science.

FOR SALE

Nuclear Power Station, complete with cooling towers, central core and generators. Fully quaranteed, £30 million, or near offer. Easy terms available.

Phone 01-237-9261 after 6 p.m.

The Common Market

Britain is a member of the European Economic Community (or EEC), known as the Common Market. The ten countries in the EEC have agreed to allow free trade amongst themselves without any *tariff barriers* – that is, without putting any taxes on each others goods that they do not put on their own goods – in order to encourage trade. Most of our trade is now done with other Common Market countries, so, since we depend so much on trade, it is clearly in our interests to be in the EEC. However, many people now think that the cost of our membership (we are obliged to buy food from Europe when we could probably get it more cheaply elsewhere) is too high, and all the major political parties are pledged to try and reduce our contributions to Europe.

Other countries we trade with a lot are the United States, Canada, the European countries not in the EEC, Australia, and South Africa.

Our overseas trade in 1979			
	billion		
	Imports	Exports	Balance
Manufacturing	31.4	33.1	+ 1.7
Fuel	5.8	4.3	− 1.5
Food, drink, tobacco	6.5	2.9	− 3.6
Raw Materials	4.0	1.2	− 2.8
Invisibles	20.8	22.3	+ 1.5

Source: Annual Abstract of Statistics 1981

NB £billion means thousands of millions of pounds

Questions

Head this section 'Foreign trade', and answer the following questions.
1 What is an *export*?
2 Why is Britain so dependent on foreign trade?
3 Even if we could produce enough food for everyone ourselves, we would still want to import food. Why? Give five examples of foods we are unable to grow in Britain.
4 Why does it make any difference to us how much the pound is worth in foreign currency, even if we never go abroad?
5 Take *five* of the types of thing Britain sells to other countries, and against each name one company you know of which makes that product.
6 The ships which carry our exports and imports form the Merchant Navy (as opposed to the Royal Navy which comprises our fighting ships). Britain has a much larger Merchant Navy that most other countries. Can you suggest why this is so? Can you go on from this to suggest why until sixty years ago Britain had the largest fighting Navy in the world?
7 Why is it in our interests to belong to the EEC?
8 Can you name the other nine countries in the EEC? The initial letters of their names are: F_____, W_____ G_____, B_____ , L_____, N_____, D_____, E_____, G_____, and I_____.
If your teacher can give you a blank map of Europe and an atlas, you can mark the ten EEC countries and their capital cities on the map.

Homework

1 Find ten articles in your home which were made abroad. List them, with the name of the firm which made them, and their country of origin.
2 Watch the news, or look in the paper, and find out how many US dollars the pound is worth.
3 Some British shops now have branches abroad to sell British goods directly to foreigners. You can often tell which they are because their labels are printed in languages other than English. Have you or your parents bought anything from such a shop recently?

11

Sources of power

Power and energy

We have seen that many machines need power, or energy, to work them, because they are too big or too heavy to be worked by human muscles alone. Indeed, *energy* is one of the four things a factory needs to run its processes (along with *labour*, *capital* and *enterprise* – see Chapter 5).

Before the Industrial Revolution machines were relatively light and simple, and their power came from harnessing *animals*, the *wind*, or *water*.

Even at the start of the Industrial Revolution, the early factories used water-wheels to power their first machines. However as machines got heavier, larger and faster, and as they started to be made from iron, new and stronger power sources were required. During the 19th century *steam* was used as the major driving force of our machines, and it was produced by boiling water with our plentiful supplies of *coal*.

Electricity

During the 20th century electricity gradually replaced steam as the driving force of many machines. Electricity is more efficient than steam (less is wasted inside the machine), and is much easier to carry around the factory (by using wires). It also produces less pollution, and it was the building of the London Underground that really introduced electric power to Britain. Another common driving force in many factories is *compressed air*, which although it needs pipes to carry it around the factory is very powerful.

Compressed air, electricity and steam are all forms of energy, but they are not power *sources*, because they all need to be manufactured, or produced, from something else. Steam is produced by boiling water, using anything which will burn, like coal or gas. Electricity is produced in a generator.

The generator

A generator is a large cylinder with an axle going through it, containing coils of wire and magnets. Precisely how it works is not important here, although you may learn about it in science, but when the axle is turned quickly, electricity is produced. So something is needed to turn the axle. The dynamo or alternator in a car is a small generator, and the axle in that is turned by the fan belt connected to the engine.

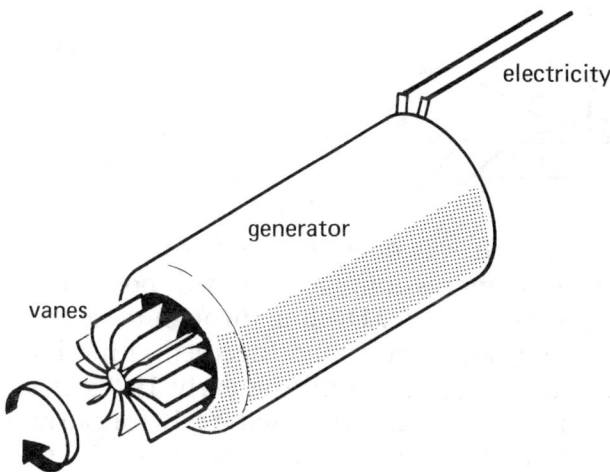

electricity

generator

vanes

In a power station the generators are much bigger, and have vanes fitted to the end of the axle, forming a *turbine*. This turbine is turned either by *steam*, or by fast flowing *water*.

Electricity produced from water is called *hydro-electricity*. A dam is built at the top of a hill, and water travels from the dam down the hill in pipes to the turbine at the bottom. By the time the water reaches the turbine it is moving fast enough to turn the generator and produce electricity. It is only in mountainous areas that hydro-electric generation is possible, and Britain produces very little of her electricity in this way.

Steam generation

The vast majority of our electricity is generated by using steam to turn the turbines. Heat is needed to boil water to produce the steam, and this heat comes from three main sources – coal, oil, and nuclear fuel.

Coal is a *fossil fuel*. This means it was once alive, in the form of plants, but over millions of years has been compressed into the form in which we now use it. Britain has a great deal of coal, and is one of the world's major producers. So it is natural that most of our power stations use coal to make their steam. Coal mining is a primary industry.

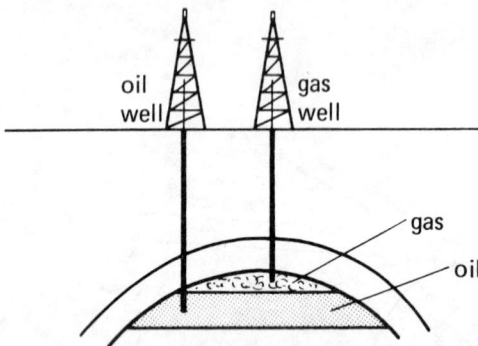

oil well   gas well   gas   oil

Oil, too, is a fossil fuel. It was once tiny sea creatures which, after millions of years of compression, have formed 'pools' of oil trapped under certain types of rock. Drilling through these rocks releases the oil. Natural gas is often found together with oil and was produced in the same way. Up until the early 1970s cheap imported oil was readily available and was used freely for burning by industry and power stations. The oil-producing countries then enormously increased their prices which threw much of the

60

Western world into some financial chaos. One result was that it became worthwhile for Britain to start drilling for oil under the North Sea, and we now produce more than enough oil to satisfy our own needs from this source.

Nuclear fuel is based on *uranium* which is a *mineral*, not a fossil fuel (it was never alive). Uranium is mined in many parts of the world and only very small amounts of it are needed to produce huge quantities of heat. Once it has been processed the uranium is turned into either the very radioactive and unstable uranium '235', or into plutonium. The processing is very complex indeed and is beyond the reach of most countries. When more than a certain 'critical' amount of uranium 235 or plutonium is put together it reacts of its own accord, producing great heat. If left uncontrolled it will explode (this happens in an atomic bomb). In a nuclear reactor the reaction is controlled to get the heat without the explosion, once again to turn water into steam to drive the turbines.

Nuclear reactors can be built small enough to power submarines, and because they use so little fuel and do not require air for burning, nuclear-powered submarines can remain underwater for very long periods. The Royal Navy has several such submarines.

Britain leads the world in nuclear technology and produces more electricity in nuclear reactors than any other country – 10% of our total power output. The original promises of abundant cheap electricity have not been fulfilled, however, because the technology involved has proved much more complicated and costly than expected. Theoretically, nuclear power could supply all our energy needs. A nuclear reactor uses so little fuel that the world's known deposits of uranium would last many centuries. However the substances involved are so dangerous that many people think our developments in this field should be halted.

Robbing the earth

Coal, oil and gas were made in the earth millions of years ago. The amount of them is fixed, and when it has gone there will be no more. And yet our industries and power stations are using them up at a colossal rate in their demand for heat and electricity. It is impossible to tell how long it will be before they run out, because we do not know whether, for example, other countries which are not industrial at the moment will start industries and therefore need their own energy. Even if world demand for energy only increases as it has done over the last twenty years, we will run out of fossil fuels in the years shown below:

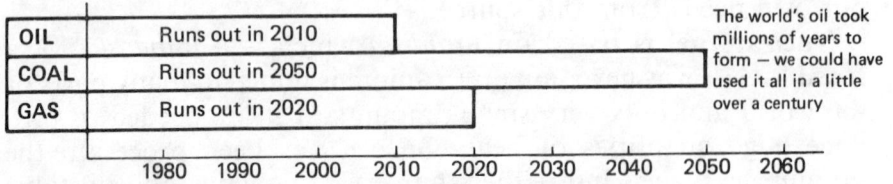

OIL	Runs out in 2010
COAL	Runs out in 2050
GAS	Runs out in 2020

The world's oil took millions of years to form — we could have used it all in a little over a century

1980 1990 2000 2010 2020 2030 2040 2050 2060

So the lights go out in 2050?

Most unlikely. As these fuels get scarcer and scarcer, so they will become more expensive. This will mean people will use less, and will look hard for new sources (like finding oil in the North Sea). So the figures given above are certainly too pessimistic. And the search will be on (many people say we should be doing more of this already) to find *alternative* sources of power. Many things will burn, but only oil can easily provide plastics and petrol. So it seems a bit crazy to waste this precious and scarce fuel in burning.

Alternative sources of power

The fossil fuels are called *finite* sources of power because they will run out (fairly soon). Let us look at some *renewable* sources of power which can never run out.

Solar power
We can use the sun's rays to heat water into steam. Experiments are going on with various mirrors and lenses to do this. Or we can save electricity by using solar panels to heat our water at home. Or we can get electricity directly from sunlight by using the special panels satellites have to power them in space.

Problems? What happens at night, or on a cloudy day? And it requires a panel one metre square to produce enough power to light a single light bulb on a sunny day!

The wind and the waves
Water is already used to produce electricity in hydro-electric power stations. And wind can drive generators directly. But whereas the generator stops when the wind drops, the *tides* never stop, and ways are being looked at of making the tides turn the generators.

Geothermal energy
In several parts of the world underground water is boiled by the heat in the earth's crust. Where this occurs it can be used to produce electricity, and does so notably in Italy and New Zealand.

The trouble with renewable energy sources is that they are either unreliable (like the wind), cannot be stored (like sunlight), or are likely to be prohibitively expensive (like wave power). Nuclear fuel, although technically a finite power source, is one answer if the dangers and technological difficulties can be overcome. And in the long run we will probably find out how to gather some of the energy from the sun which is now lost in space.

Questions

Write the title 'Power' in your workbook.

1 What were the main sources of power before the Industrial Revolution?
2 During the Industrial Revolution steam became a common form of energy. Which fuel was used to produce the steam?
3 What is a *finite* power source? List three.
4 What is a *renewable* power source? List three.
5 Why do we need to look for new sources of power?
6 The production of electricity is an example of *manufacturing industry*; electricity is made in factories called power stations. Which raw materials are used, and what processes are involved in its manufacture?
7 What are the advantages and disadvantages of the use of nuclear fuel to produce electricity?

12

The new technology – chips with everything!

Billy: 'What's for lunch today?'
Susan: 'Fish fingers and chips.'
Billy: 'I like chips with everything!'

No, we are not going to talk about chips made from potatoes, you can see your Home Economics teacher to find out how to do that! We are going to talk about chips made from silicon – silicon chips.

Billy: 'What's silicon?'
Susan: 'After oxygen, the most common element on earth. All sand, all soil, and most rocks contain silicon. Altogether, a quarter of the earth's crust is silicon.'
Billy: 'So what's a silicon chip?'
Susan: 'I haven't the remotest idea, but I know there's one in my digital watch, and one in your calculator.'

The new technology

Technology is using inventions and machines to help improve production. As we have seen, there was an enormous advance in technology during the Industrial Revolution with the invention and use of the steam engine, metal machinery, and the power and heat from coal and gas. Since then, technology has continued to advance, but more slowly, with the development of the internal combustion engine, the aeroplane, and electricity. However we are now in the middle, or perhaps at the beginning, of another very rapid period of advancement with the development of technology based on the *silicon chip*. This silicon chip technology is sometimes referred to as the *new technology*, and is beginning to have a big effect on how we live and work.

'So what's a silicon chip?'

When computers were first built in the late 1940s, they used thousands of *valves* all joined with wires. A valve looks a bit like a thin light bulb, and these early computers were very large and very expensive. They could do a lot of calculations very quickly, however, and could store and manipulate huge quantities of information. So the search was on to make them smaller and cheaper. This was partly achieved by the invention of the *transistor*, which does much the same as a valve, but is much smaller, is not made of glass, and uses less electricity. Transistors enabled small battery powered radios to be made for the first time.

Radio valves

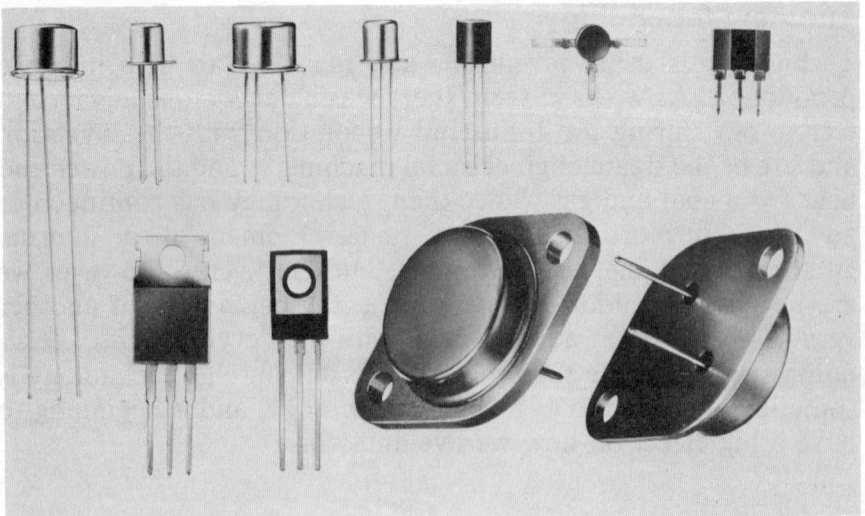

Typical transistor encapsulations

The real breakthrough came, however, when it was discovered that not only transistors, but also whole circuits of wires could be 'printed' ('etched' is a closer description of the process) onto wafer-thin slices of silicon. These slices of silicon, with their printed circuits and connectors are the so called 'silicon chips', sometimes called 'microprocessers'.

Nowadays, tens of thousands of transistors and related circuitry can be printed on to a slice of silicon the size of your thumbnail. Not only are these micro-processors much smaller than previous computers, they are also much, much cheaper. Although the printing is very complicated and relies upon, amongst other things, the bombarding of the slice of silicon with atomic particles, chips can be mass produced in great numbers, and the basic raw material – silicon – is very common, and therefore cheap.

You can now hold in your hand the processing unit for a computer which fifteen years ago would have taken up a whole room and cost literally hundreds of thousands of pounds.

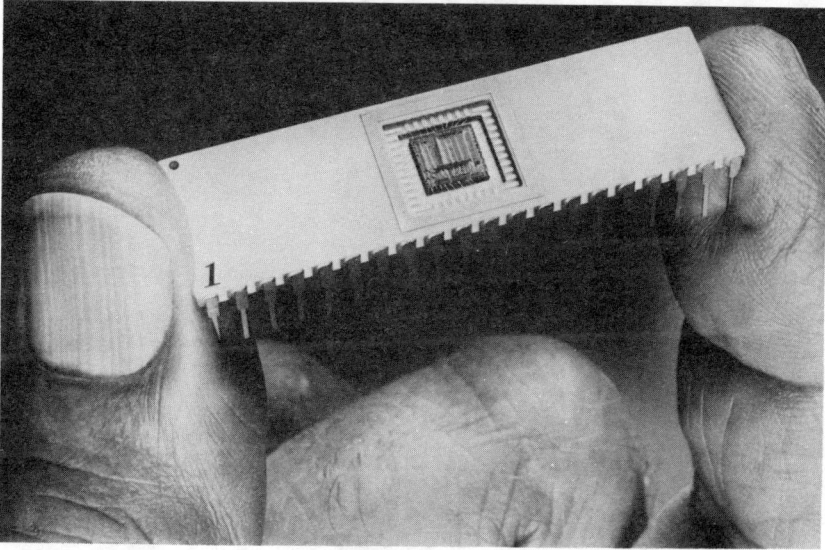

The Ferranti F100-L microprocessor

What do they do?

1 Control machinery

Think of a chip as a collection of switches which can be turned on and off in any order thousands of times per second, in accordance with any plan you care to give it. This plan can either be built into the chip, or fed in later while you are operating it, and is called the chip's *program*. Using these switches, the chip can *control* any machinery it is wired up to. Because of the huge number of switches, and the speed at which they work, a chip can control much more complicated machinery much more accurately than a human operator could.

Example . . . .

When playing a 'space invaders' machine you press the 'fire' button. The machine's micro-processor, or chip, then operates all the appropriate lights, sounds and scoring devices in the right order. It is controlling all the parts of the machine in a pre-determined manner, relating to what the machine was showing when you pressed the button. Not only is it more complicated than the old 'pin-ball' machines, but it can be held in your hand! (Try putting a 'pin-ball' machine in your pocket!)

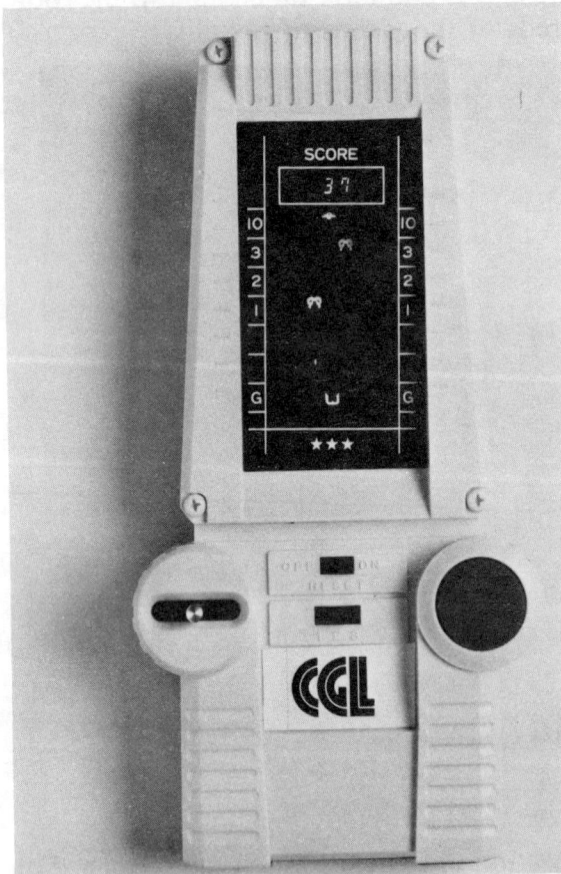

The Galaxy Invader, Computer Games Ltd

2 Store information

There are many millions of different positions for the switches in a chip, and each position can be made to stand for a particular letter or number. So chips can 'remember' pieces of information, and can then sort, store or compare them.

What use are they?

They are incredibly useful. Every machine which needs controlling can be controlled more accurately with a microprocessor. Among existing machines which have been adapted to 'chip control' are deep freezers, ovens, washing machines, sewing machines, cash registers, packing machines, central heating systems, car ignition systems and televisions.

But much more important is their use in machines which were too complicated to work at all without the chip's ability to control or remember, and could not be made small or cheap enough using old-style computers.

We describe a few 'new technology' inventions of the 1970's below.

Calculators

Among the first of the new inventions, we hardly need to mention the effect calculators have had. And remember that in 1970 *they did not exist*.

The Hewlett-Packard 38C calculator

Word processors

A word processor is a bit like a typewriter, only when the operator types, the letters come up in a row of lights, and are then transferred to paper using ink jets at incredible speed. Whole sentences or even pages can be remembered by the machine and typed at the press of one key. Part of a letter can be typed automatically, and then the machine will stop for a single word, perhaps a person's name, to be inserted by the operator to make the letter look personal. One machine can do the work of a whole team of typists.

Robots

One of the most important new inventions is the industrial robot. Forget about eight foot high metal men with ray guns and electronic voices – industrial robots are built to do one job only, and look rather like boxes with one long arm. The arm can be controlled (by the microprocessor) to move to any position and then

The robot weld body production, British Leyland, Longbridge

lift something, move it, or work a hand-held machine, like a spot-welder, a paint spray, a glass cutter, or a drill. The majority of robots work to an accuracy of 1 mm, but they can be made even more precise.

'Talking' machines

The most recent inventions use the chip to control 'voice synthesizers' which mimic the human voice and can talk to you. One such device can read print with a camera and convert it to speech. (To help blind people for example.) Others can be linked to telephones in booking offices, or even translating machines. The days of being able to talk into a microphone in English, and having your words come out of a speaker in, say, French, are not far off.

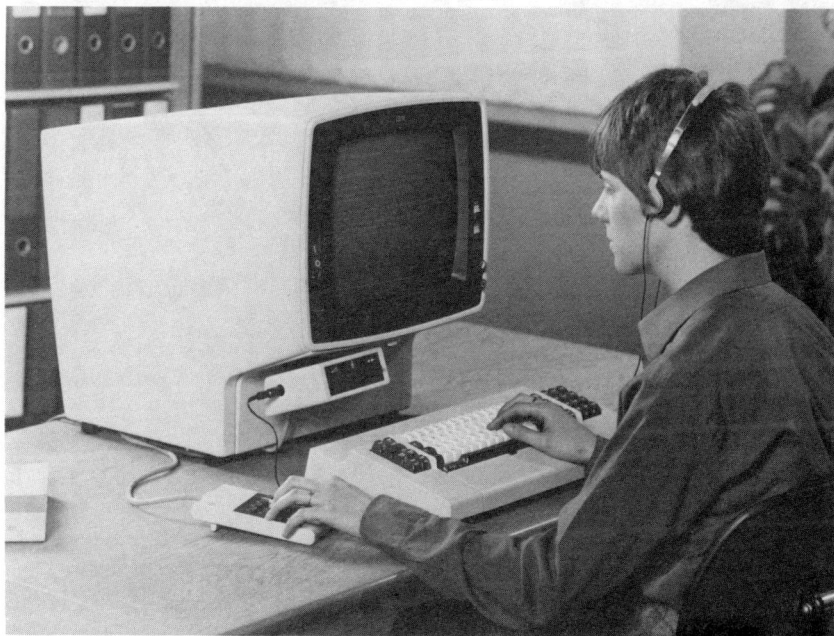

The IBM 'Talking Terminal'

Digital watches

The timer is a quartz crystal rather than a balance wheel, and control is by a chip. Unlike old style watches there are no moving parts and so accuracy up to 5 seconds a month can be achieved. The most expensive jewelled lever watches can get nowhere near this accuracy.

Seiko Time (UK) Ltd

Toys and games

These break down into three groups: calculator-type games, like spelling or arithmetic games; video or TV games; and model games, like controlling a model car with a hand held ultra sonic device. All share the requirement of a chip to control their many functions. In fact before the invention of the chip, the electronics needed to control the model car would hardly have fitted into a double decker bus!

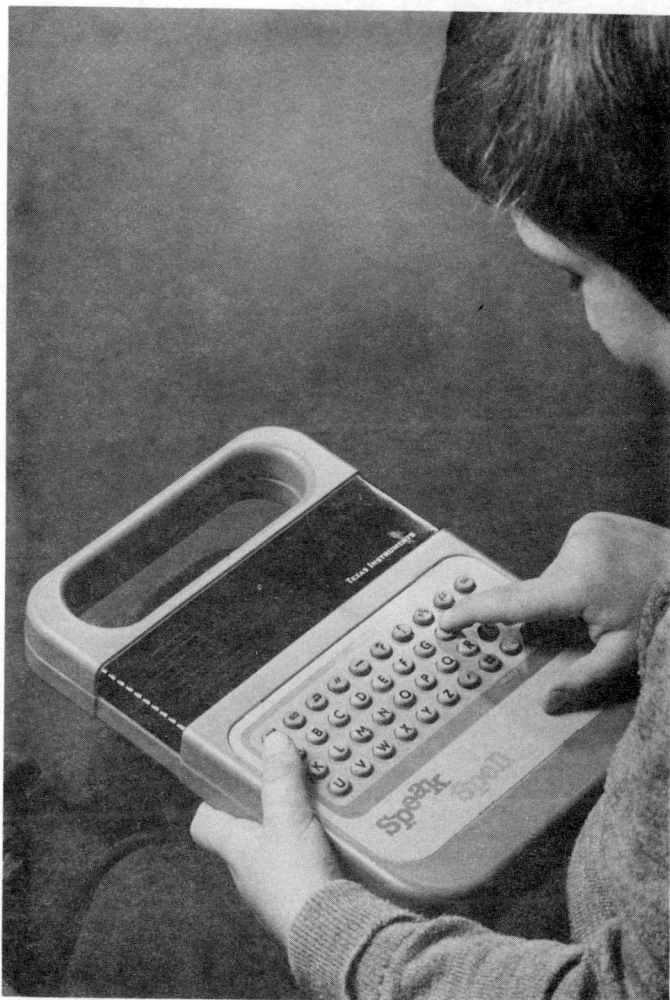

Speak and Spell, Texas Instruments

THINK

When Neil Armstrong stepped on the moon in 1969, he would not have understood the technology behind a digital watch – they had not yet been invented.

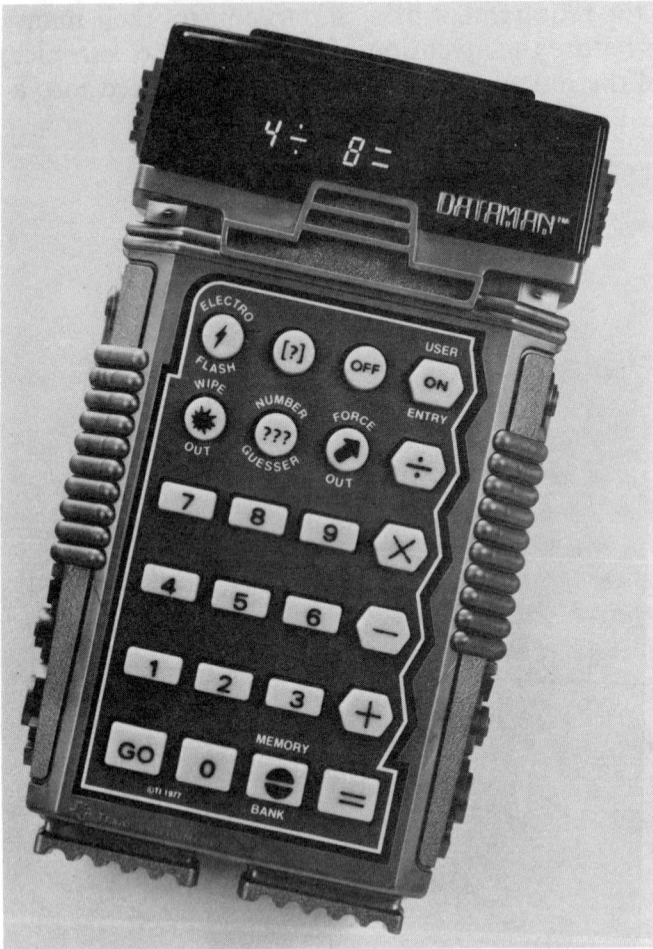

Dataman, Texas Instruments

Questions

Write the title 'The new technology' in your workbook.

1 What is a silicon chip?
2 What two things can a silicon chip do?
3 What advantages do industrial robots have over human workers?
4 Is the development of the new technology likely to lead to more people being employed in manufacturing industry, or less?

   Give examples of the types of job which could be replaced by microprocessors or robots, and those extra jobs which microprocessors will bring.

5 Choose the *three* inventions based on the silicon chip we have described which you think are the biggest advances. Describe them and say why you picked them.

6 What things do you have at home controlled by silicon chips?

7 *'Journey into the future'*. Imagine you are living in Britain in the year 2025. You can either be yourself at the age you will be then, or a young person just leaving school. Describe what you think your home and job will be like then. Start like this: 'I stretched lazily as the alarm sounded. . . .'

13

Trade unions

'Everyone out!'

Hardly a day seems to go by without the newspapers or television mentioning a strike of workers in one firm or another. Sometimes such a strike has a dramatic effect on people, like stopping the buses or trains running, causing power cuts, or closing the schools. More often a strike affects few people directly, other than those involved with the firm concerned. People who are not on strike are often quick to blame the trade unions for any loss or inconvenience they suffer.

This is rather a one-sided view of unions, however. Strikes get reported because they are newsworthy, but there are not nearly as many of them as one might imagine. In fact, in a normal *year*, the average time lost through strikes is *under an hour* for each worker. This is far, far less than the time lost through other causes, like illness.

Working normally: 11 months, 30 days, 7 hours, 10 minutes	On strike 50 minutes

And many millions of workers have never been on strike at all in their whole working lives.

What is a strike?

A strike is when a group of workers refuse to work, either because they are unhappy with their pay or conditions, or because they feel the management of the firm has been acting very unfairly. When workers are on strike, their firm does not pay them any wages, so they lose their pay. Also, since nothing is being made, the firm loses money too. And if the business is one used by members of the public (like the buses), they will suffer loss and inconvenience as well. So everyone loses during a strike, which is why going on strike is a last resort, and rather rare.

Because of this, trade unions try and avoid strikes. Most strikes are 'unofficial', or 'widcat', which means they are not supported by the union.

But occasionally, the union will agree that a strike is the only way left to solve a problem, or dispute, and the strike then becomes 'official', and the union gives its members who are on strike a small amount of strike pay. Note that people who are on strike cannot claim any money for themselves from the Department of Health and Social Security, only for their families.

So what do unions do?

They negotiate. A union is an organization of workers, either in one particular industry, or across a group of different industries. The workers each pay a small subscription and the union then employs *officials* to talk to the employers on the workers' behalf. These officials are skilled at sorting out problems, and save workers having to disagree with their own employer. They talk about wages, holidays, conditions at work (whether a factory is too hot or too cold, or an office too crowded), safety and training. They offer their members advice about compensation for accidents or sickness, and before the state retirement pension came into being they used to pay pensions to retired workers, or workers' dependents.

Because the union official represents a lot of people, he or she has a lot more influence with the firm than a single worker.

The shop steward

Often the members of a union in one particular firm will elect one of their number to be their shop steward. He or she will represent their views to the management of the firm about minor matters which can be dealt with without the need for a union official.

Why strike?

Very occasionally, the negotiations break down when the union officials and the management of the firm simply cannot agree, perhaps about a pay claim. There is then very little the workers can do except take *industrial action* to try and persuade the firm to change its mind. Even at this point there is a way out, though.

There is an independent body called ACAS (the Advisory Conciliation and Arbitration Service) which, if both parties ask, will look into a dispute and suggest a compromise. You may have heard the expression 'going to arbitration'.

Industrial action is much more likely if the workers do not trust the management, or the management will not negotiate at all, and some firms over the years fall into a pattern of mutual mistrust and consequent industrial action.

Industrial action

The *go-slow*. This is where workers do their normal job, but do it much more slowly than usual, so less is produced. It is similar to the *work-to-rule* where the workers follow every little rule to the letter, thereby taking much longer than usual to do everything. Also used is the *overtime ban*, when workers refuse to work any longer than their standard (usually eight hour) day. And finally, there is the *strike*.

Too much power?

Unions only have the power their members give them – they are groups of ordinary people. And very few people in this country would say that workers should not be able to strike if they are very unhappy with their firm; after all striking is a last resort, and the workers themselves lose money by it as well as the firm. Certainly the union gives a worker far more power than he or she would have on his or her own, but by doing so it protects the worker from the whim of an unscrupulous or mean employer.

But there are some ways in which unions can have power over people who have nothing to do with them or the firm they work for.

1 Political power

Although ten million people are members of trade unions, this is less than half the workforce, and only a fifth of the country as a whole. Yet the unions have a very big say in the policies of the Labour Party, and hence the government when Labour is in power. This is because the unions pay most of the Labour Party's expenses, through the *political levy* which most union members pay as part of their subscription. Members do not have to pay this levy, but many of them do not know this.

Some people think it is unfair that relatively few people should have this large say, but others think that it is right that the views of ordinary working people should be represented in government policy in this way. It is also true that many union members who complain about the political power of the unions do not themselves attend union meetings and help to form the policies.

2 Power over the public

Some workers in 'key' industries (like electricity generation) can cause immense harm to people who have nothing to do with the dispute when they strike. A very few workers (like the police) are not allowed to go on strike for this reason, but some people think many more should be included, perhaps hospital workers, miners, and power workers. On the other hand, what would these workers then do if they did have a serious grievance?

3 Picketting

Picketting is when a group of workers on strike forms up outside the factory gates and tries to persuade the other workers to go on strike too. If a union member refuses, he or she is called a *blackleg*. So long as the picket is peaceful this is quite legal and acceptable, but sometimes the strikers picket other factories (perhaps their firm's supplier or customer) and try and stop their workers working. This is called *secondary picketting*, and some people think it is unfair both on the other firm and its workers.

4 The closed shop

In a 'closed shop' all the workers in a particular place of employment have to belong to a union if they are to keep their job. This is an agreement between the union and the firm. The argument in favour of closed shops is that everyone benefits from the union's negotiations, so everyone should support the union. On the other hand, perhaps people should be free to decide whether they want to join the union or not.

The law and unions

During the 19th century people fought long and hard to win the right to strike and form unions, sometimes being sent to prison for their pains. The result is that unions have a special place in the law, and firms now have to give a fair deal to their workers in terms of pay and conditions. Opinion changes about whether some of the unions' powers are right or wrong, however, and governments periodically pass laws over such matters as those raised above. In many countries it is still illegal to belong to a union or to go on strike, whatever the reason, such as in some of the South American countries, and until recently even in Spain and Greece.

The TUC

Each year representatives of the different unions meet together in the Trade Union Congress to discuss matters which concern them all. Throughout the year the TUC sorts out problems between unions, and represents the union point of view to the government.

Things to do

1 What is a trade union?
2 What is the difference between a shop steward and a union official?
3 Imagine you are a shop steward, and have been asked by your fellow union members to go and see the personnel manager and ask for an extra week's holiday for everyone this year. What arguments might you use to support the claim?
   If you were the personnel manager, what arguments might you use to persuade the shop steward that the extra holiday was not a good idea?
4 What different forms of industrial action are there?
5 What do you think of: closed shops; secondary picketting; forbidding certain groups of workers to go on strike? (Who would you include?)
6 The five biggest unions are the TGWU, the AUEW, the GMWU, NALGO and NUPE. Can you find out what each of these initials stands for, and what types of workers each represents?

14

Taxation and government spending

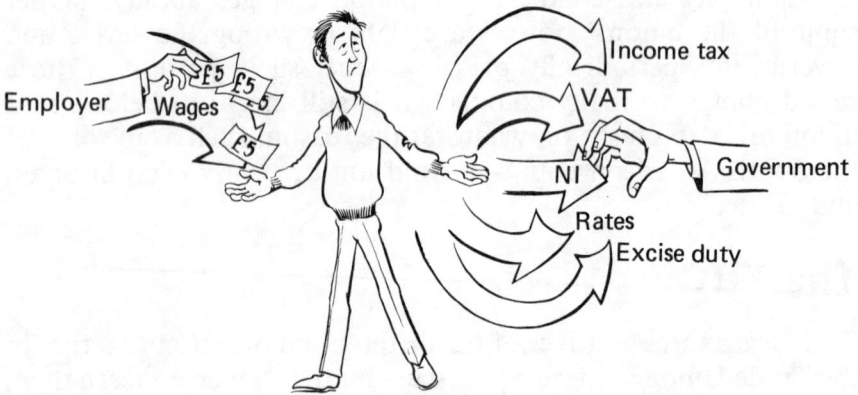

We all use schools, doctors, hospitals and the roads. The country has an Army, Navy and Air Force to protect it, and a police force to uphold the law. Each house has its dustbins emptied, is connected to the water supply and, in most cases, to the drainage system. People who have retired or are too sick to work collect pensions, and parents receive child benefit each month for their children.

In most cases these services are provided free of charge, but they still cost money. Some are paid for by the government, and some by local authorities, and the money to provide them comes from the money we pay in rates and taxes. Altogether they add up to an enormous amount of money. In fact, just about half of all the money spent in Britain is spent by government and local authorities.

Tax

Tax is money paid by people to the government, and falls into two groups. *Direct* tax is tax paid out of what we earn, usually before we get paid, and *indirect* tax is tax paid on things we buy.

There are two main direct taxes, income tax and National Insurance.

Income tax

A person is charged income tax on what he or she earns, wherever it comes from, at a basic rate of 30 pence in the pound (30%). But you do not pay income tax on all your earnings. You are allowed to earn a certain amount (called your *allowances*) before you pay tax. The allowances for a single person for 1982 are £1565 (£30 per week), and for a married man £2445 (£45 per week).

To work out how much tax you will pay each week, take your allowances off your total pay (called your *gross* pay) and multiply the number of pounds left by 30p each.

Complications

In practice, your employer deducts your tax each time you are paid, and sends the money to the Inland Revenue. You have a *code number* which shows what your allowances are and by looking at tax tables the amount of tax due can be calculated. Your yearly allowances are ten times your code number, so with a single person's allowances your code number will be 156. Since your allowances are spread over the tax year, which runs from 6 April to the next 5 April, if you do not work all of this time you will pay less tax when you do work to compensate. This method of tax collection is PAYE (Pay As You Earn). The amount of tax a person pays goes up to 40p in the pound if they earn over £12 800 a year, and continues to rise for higher earners. Your allowances can alter according to your circumstances, which is why you fill in a *tax return* each year. The basic allowances and the rate of tax can change each year, usually in the Budget.

Example of income tax
Gross Pay: £70.45
Take off allowances: £70.45 − £30 = £40.45
Multiply number of pounds left by 30p = 40 × 30p = £12
So you will pay £12 tax.

National Insurance

Unlike income tax, there are no allowances for National Insurance. Everyone who earns more than £29 per week (1982 figure) pays 8¾% of all their pay in National Insurance. This, too, is deducted by the employer. There is a maximum amount a person can pay each week, however, which is currently £17.50. In our example above of gross weekly pay of £70.45, the National Insurance would be £70 × 8¾% = £6.13.

GROSS PAY: £70.45
DEDUCTIONS:
 INCOME TAX: £12.00
 NI : £6.13
  TOTAL : £18.13
NET PAY (what you get): £52.32

Indirect taxes

The main taxes we pay on what we spend are VAT (Value Added Tax), and excise duties.

VAT is charged on most goods (but not food or children's clothing) and services, and is, in 1982, 15% of the price. It is usually included in the advertised price of goods in shops, but not for some services (like garage repair work). When comparing prices you should always make sure that the VAT is included.

Excise duties are extra taxes paid on some things on top of VAT. Alcohol and tobacco are the main items concerned.
You can see why these items can be bought much more cheaply at 'duty free' shops where there is no excise duty!

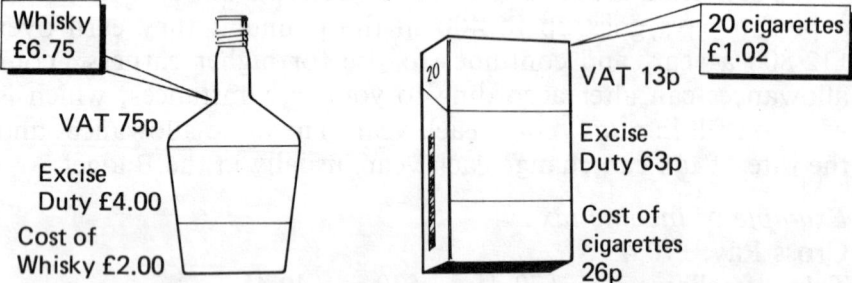

Whisky £6.75
VAT 75p
Excise Duty £4.00
Cost of Whisky £2.00

20 cigarettes £1.02
VAT 13p
Excise Duty 63p
Cost of cigarettes 26p

Special extra taxes are also paid when buying certain other goods, including cars, and petrol and oil. You will know there is also the *road fund tax* to pay when you own a car, currently £80 per year. This is the 'tax disc' on a car's windscreen.

Rates

Local authorities, being Metropolitan and County Councils, District and Borough, Regional and Islands Councils, pay for schools, housing, some roads, water, sewage, refuse disposal, parks, and towards the cost of the buses. Roughly half of their money comes in grants from the government. The rest is paid for by the *rates*. Every house is given a *rateable value*, which reflects how much rent could be charged if the house was let to someone. It is more if the house has central heating, is bigger, has more rooms, and so on. The local authority works out how much money it needs to run the services, and then fixes a *rate*, which is the proportion of the rateable value each house will pay for the year. It is given as so much in every pound of rateable value.

Example of rates
Rateable value of house: £400
Rate for the year: 96p in the pound
Rates paid: $400 \times 96p = £384$

Many people think rates are an unfair tax. It is possible to get a *rebate*, which means being let off some of your rates if you have a low income, but apart from this rates are the only tax which takes no account of a person's ability to afford it. A person living on their own pays the same rates as a family of four wage earners living in a similar house next door. Firms, too, pay rates on all their buildings.

Company taxes

As well as rates, firms pay tax on their profits. This is called *corporation tax*. They also pay an extra *National Insurance* contribution for each of their employees, on top of what the employee pays, which is at the moment 13.7% of the wages.

Where the money comes from

Sources of central and local government revenue 1979:

Income tax and
corporation tax: £25 billion

National
Insurance: £11½ billion

VAT, excise
duties and rates: £30½ billion   Total £75 billion

Council house
rents: £2½ billion

Various other
taxes (betting
duty, capital
gains tax, land
tax etc): £5½ billion

Source: National Income and
Expenditure 1980

Where the money goes

Out of every £1 the government and local authorities spend, this much goes on:

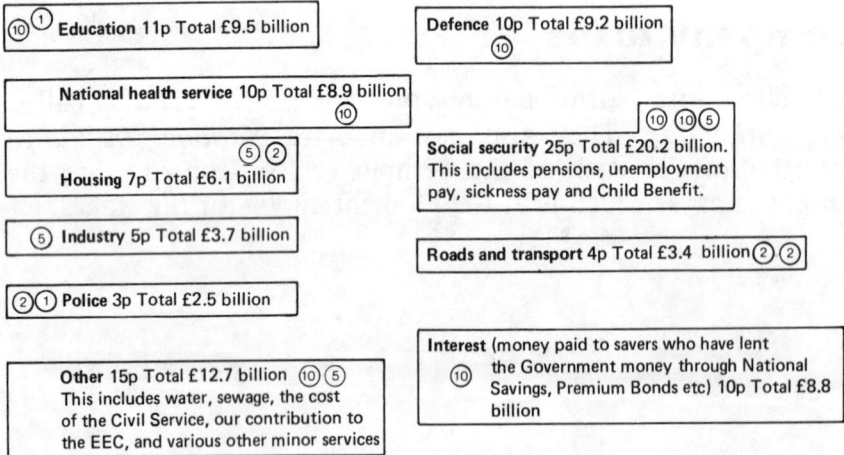

WHERE THE MONEY GOES

Out of every £1 the government and local authorities spend, this much goes on:

⑩① Education 11p Total £9.5 billion

Defence 10p Total £9.2 billion ⑩

National health service 10p Total £8.9 billion ⑩

⑤② Housing 7p Total £6.1 billion

Social security 25p Total £20.2 billion. ⑩⑩⑤
This includes pensions, unemployment pay, sickness pay and Child Benefit.

⑤ Industry 5p Total £3.7 billion

Roads and transport 4p Total £3.4 billion ②②

②① Police 3p Total £2.5 billion

Other 15p Total £12.7 billion ⑩⑤
This includes water, sewage, the cost of the Civil Service, our contribution to the EEC, and various other minor services

Interest (money paid to savers who have lent ⑩ the Government money through National Savings, Premium Bonds etc) 10p Total £8.8 billion

Cost of running Britain
£85,000 million

Income from taxes
£75,000 million

Result? Borrowing
£10,000 million

If you add the figures up, you will see they come to £85 billion. This is £10 billion less than the money raised from taxes, and the Government had to borrow the extra from savers to 'balance its books'.

Questions

Write the title 'Taxation and government spending' in your workbook, and answer the following questions in complete sentences.

1　What is meant by 'direct taxes'?
2　What are the two main direct taxes we pay?
3　What are 'indirect taxes'?
4　Give three examples of indirect taxes.
5　What are rates, and who are they paid to?
6　Draw a 'bar graph' showing the amounts of money the government and local authorities spend out of every pound on the various services they provide. Your vertical scale should go from 0 to 25p.
　Which service costs the most?

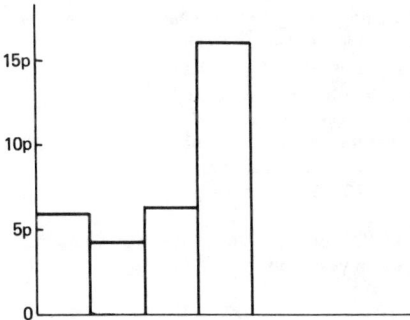

7　What is PAYE?
8　If you had to raise some extra money for the government (perhaps to cut down its borrowing) what taxes would you raise, and why?
9　Are there any taxes you would reduce or abolish because you think they are unfair?
10　Try and work out roughly how much your *net pay* would be (after deducting income tax and national insurance) if your *gross pay* was
　a)　£50 per week
　b)　£90 per week
　c)　£150 per week.

15

Inflation and unemployment

The balloon goes up

How often have you heard your parents comparing prices today with what they used to be in the past? Or saying how little pocket money they used to be given, and what they could buy with it? This increasing of prices year by year is called inflation, and over your lifetime has been really dramatic. For instance in 1967 a Mars bar cost 2p, as did a bag of crisps. A loaf of bread was under 5p, and for 50p you could buy a gallon of petrol, ten cigarettes, a pint of beer, and still have enough change for fish and chips! Some things have gone up in price more than others. Postage has gone from 1½p to 15½p – a rise of ten times, but records have only gone from 33p to £1.10, a rise of three times. It is possible, however, to take an average of the sort of things people tend to buy — a sort of shopping basket including everything from bread to bus fares — and measure how its total price changes from year to year, or month to month. This total is called the Retail Price Index, or RPI, and is worked out and published each month. Before 1970 prices had always gone up a little from year to year, but it was during the 1970s that the rises started to get really big, and in some years inflation rose to over 20%. Over the decade as a whole the Retail Price Index quadrupled, which means on average prices in 1980 were four times what they were in 1970. Of course wages had gone up a lot too.

Inflation has now dropped to around 10%, but even this means that prices will double in seven years and quadruple in fourteen.

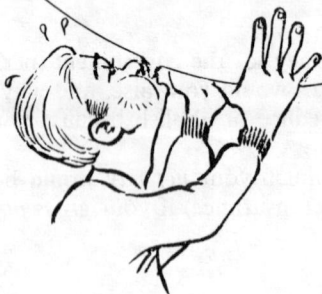

Does inflation matter?

That depends on who you are. If you are working, and your income goes up each year by the same amount as the rise in the RPI, then in one sense inflation will not affect you. However the RPI only takes an average of price rises, and what you yourself choose to buy, or have to buy (like food, housing and fuel) might have gone up by more than the average. Even if you are not working, providing whatever money you do get (like a pension) is 'index-linked' (that means it goes up each year by exactly the same amount as the RPI) you may not be unduly affected. But if your income does not rise as much as prices, or if your pension is not index-linked, you will fairly quickly suffer through inflation. And the higher inflation is, the more people there are who are likely to be in that position, and the more they will suffer.

Another problem with inflation is its effect on industry. Unless a firm constantly puts up its prices (which may stop it selling its goods), it will soon find that its raw materials cost more than the money it has been getting for its finished products. If this happens it will not make any profit and may go bankrupt. Also planning ahead is very difficult if you have no idea how much prices or wages will rise.

The inflationary spiral

Inflation tends to feed on itself, and spiral upwards. People do not want to save, because they see the value of their savings slipping away. And they want to borrow, because the money they pay back is worth less than what they borrowed. Therefore the higher inflation is, the more they spend, which pushes inflation still higher. The classic case of inflation getting completely out of control happened in Germany between the World Wars, when even postage stamps ended up costing millions of pfennigs, and people rushed out to spend all their pay as soon as they got it, before prices rose again.

Causes of inflation

The wealth of a country, as you know, is measured by the amount of goods and services produced in that country. If the amount of money in circulation (called the *money supply*) goes up without the wealth of the country increasing (which happens if people borrow more) then everything will cost more, since there is more money to share between the same amount of goods. This is called **demand** inflation.

Alternatively, if a firm pays its workers higher wages and gets the money to do so by putting up its prices rather than by increasing productivity or improving efficiency, providing people will still buy its goods this too will cause inflation. This is called **cost** inflation.

The cure?

The cure is to increase output to match any increase in the money supply, or to prevent people getting hold of the money to pay higher prices. The problem is how to do this. The government does not have complete control over the economy, and even if it did, could never be quite sure of what effect its controls were going to have. Put simply, will increasing the tax on beer raise more money for the government, or merely stop people drinking beer?

The Conservative Government elected in 1979 has tried to reduce inflation by controlling the money supply and increasing output. They have not been altogether very successful. They have certainly cut down the amount of money people have been able to spend, and this has probably kept inflation lower than it would otherwise have been. And during the same time they have caused productivity to rise – each worker is now producing more than before. But, as we saw in the last chapter, an enormous amount of spending and borrowing is done by the government itself, and strangely enough the government has been less successful in controlling this. And although each worker is producing more than previously, because there are fewer people at work, *total* production is still lower than in 1979.

Many people now think the government is trying to solve the wrong problem. It is not inflation, but unemployment that is our biggest economic worry. The government say (rightly) that the rise in unemployment is not entirely their fault, and (perhaps rightly, but perhaps not) that now industry is more efficient unemployment will soon start to fall.

Unemployment

Prime Minister Margaret Thatcher

People go to work for a lot of reasons, not all of them to do with money. They want to spend their time in a useful and constructive way; they want to help the community; and they want to exercise their skills and abilities. Some people do these things without getting paid – mothers bringing up their children, people doing voluntary work, or people engaging in their hobbies. Do you think Sir Edmund Hillary climbed Mount Everest because he was paid to be an explorer?

On the other hand, everyone wants to share in the wealth of our society, and at the moment, unless you are too old or too young to work, this usually means having a job to provide the money for you and your family to buy the things you want and need.

Ideally, there should be a job available for everyone who wants one. This does not mean everyone will always be at work. Some people will choose not to work, and others will be temporarily unemployed while they are 'between jobs'. In the first case the numbers are usually very small, and 'Employment Exchanges' (now Jobcentres) were set up in 1910 to help those in the second category.

Between 1945 and 1970 this accounted for practically everyone who was unemployed (about half a million people) – there were effectively jobs for everyone. However since 1970 unemployment has risen well beyond this level, and there are now more people unemployed in Britain (some 3 million) than ever before, most of whom want very much to work, but cannot find jobs.

Causes and cures

The cause of present unemployment is partly a decline in traditional industries, and partly cheap competition from abroad, but mainly a general low level of demand for goods and services in the country, and indeed the world, as a whole. The decline started in 1973 when the price of imported oil increased dramatically. In the past, governments have overcome such low demand by increasing their own spending, and encouraging other people to increase theirs, to build up demand for goods. However as we have seen, when this was tried in the 1970s it only led to high inflation, and the government does not want to make the same mistake again.

An alternative is to increase demand by making goods *cheaper*. This can be done by increasing productivity so that each worker makes more goods. In the short term this does not help unemployment – quite the opposite – but it might do eventually. During the Industrial Revolution the new machines led to a lot of people being made *redundant* (no longer needed by a particular factory), but enormously increased employment as a whole both by increasing the demand for the new, cheaper goods, and by increasing the wealth of the country which caused a rise in employment in other spheres. In general, increased automation leads to fewer jobs in the factory concerned at the time, but more jobs eventually, both in factories and, more especially, in service industries.

Questions

Write the title 'Inflation and unemployment' in your workbook.
1   What is inflation?
2   Why is it not a good idea to save money in a teapot under your bed?
3   Can you name three jobs which people do without getting paid?
4   What does it mean if someone is 'between jobs'?
5   Why does the government not reduce unemployment by encouraging people to spend more money to buy more goods?
6   Why does inflation 'feed on itself' to produce still higher inflation?
7   Do you think it is worth putting up with higher inflation if this means lower unemployment? Say why, or why not.
8   What is index-linking? See if you can find examples of payments or interest rates which are index-linked.